Professor Letham has gathered together  individuals through whom God has don the truth of the Gospel. With careful se assessments the reader is blessed with many historical insights into both God's sovereignty over the stage of history on the one hand and His particular interventions into the lives of the men through whom the course of that history was changed. This is a great book for any Christian who wants to know more about how God has preserved the gospel for them in the face of seemingly overwhelming odds.

David A. Hohne,
Lecturer of Theology, Philosophy and Church History,
Moore Theological College, Sydney

It has been said that ideas change the world. Actually, it is people gripped by the ideas that do the changing, as this series of studies of various Christians who did indeed change their worlds reminds us. An extremely interesting and helpful book.

Michael A. G. Haykin,
Professor of Church History and Biblical Spirituality,
The Southern Baptist Theological Seminary, Louisville, Kentucky

Weaving together biography and theology, Letham's *Gamechangers* shows us once again how fascinating Christian history can be, and how one life can influence generations to come.

Joel R. Beeke,
President,
Puritan Reformed Theological Seminary, Grand Rapids, Michigan

More than a gallery of portraits of influential characters of the Christian past, *Gamechangers* is a journey into Church history through a carefully selected list of theologians and leaders who have shaped their time and subsequent generations. From Athanasius to Karl Barth, through the Fathers, the Schoolmen, the Reformers and some modern theologians, the reader is helped to appreciate the richness and complexity of the "cloud of witnesses" that surround us. Prof. Letham is at his best when dealing with the contribution of each theologian, wisely weighting both strengths and shortcomings. On the whole *Gamechangers* is an intriguing guide to some outstanding figures of the past by one of the most articulate Reformed theological voices of our time.

Leonardo De Chirico,
Lecturer of Historical Theology,
Istituto di Formazione Evangelica e Documentazione, Padova, Italy;

ROBERT LETHAM

GAMECHANGERS

KEY FIGURES OF
THE CHRISTIAN CHURCH

CHRISTIAN
FOCUS

In memoriam
Charles Toler

Copyright © Robert Letham 2015

paperback ISBN 978-1-78191-599-8
epub ISBN 978-1-78191-624-7
mobi ISBN 978-1-78191-625-4

Published in 2015
by
Christian Focus Publications Ltd.,
Geanies House, Fearn, Ross-shire,
IV20 1TW, Scotland, Great Britain.
www.christianfocus.com

Cover design by Daniel Van Straaten

Printed by
Bell and Bain, Glasgow

CONTENTS

INTRODUCTION

These chapters were originally a series of lectures delivered at the Christian Studies Forum at the church where I was Senior Minister from 1989 to 2006, Emmanuel Orthodox Presbyterian Church, Wilmington, Delaware. The Forum began in 1993 and lasted until my departure at the end of 2006. This particular series of lectures began in 1996.

The Forum met several times a year on a Saturday morning, and consisted of a superb home cooked breakfast, a lecture by a distinguished visiting scholar—of whom there were many available between Philadelphia and Washington, DC—or myself, followed by discussion. One notable visiting lecturer described it as the best discussion group he had ever attended. There were many research chemists in the area, Wilmington being a centre of research, together with a range of intelligent laypeople, and occasional ministers, all with a keen interest in theology and the Christian faith. Public discussion frequently lasted for up to an hour after the lecture had ended.

The chapters focus on a number of figures who, for the most part, played a crucial role in the spread of the gospel and the advancement of the church. We consider briefly the life and work of each one, refer to their strengths and weaknesses, and provide some hints for further reading. As you will gather, this will be of particular interest to laypeople with a serious interest in learning of the way the church has understood the gospel down the centuries, and should also appeal to ministers and students. It is intended too to provide the reader with guidance for further study. Only one of the dozen may not fit the category of 'key figures'; John Nevin was a relatively obscure German Reformed theologian of the nineteenth century. Nonetheless, he is of much interest, particularly in North America, and has become the focus of increased attention more recently.

It is my pleasant task to thank all who have helped in the production of this book. Philip Ross encouraged its publication while Willie Mackenzie kept a watchful eye over its progress.

Behind all this I want to remember all who assisted in the Christian Studies Forum, without which these chapters would not have been produced. †Dick and Ann Symons set the room up, Ann serving her delicious breakfasts that were so much of an attraction. Jim Wadsworth took care of the funds and advised on our plans. †Dr. John Van Dyk was a generous supporter of the Forum and of other conferences held by the church on the interaction of Christianity and particular areas of life.

Above all, we recall the work of †Charles and Bertie Toler whose combined energies were responsible for it taking place originally as the Truth and Grace Breakfast Club until their move to North Carolina on 31 July 1997. It was largely Charles Toler's vision, energy, and enthusiasm that helped the ministry to get off the ground and so to flourish over this extended period of time. It is to his memory that this book is dedicated.

Robert Letham
The second week in Trinity, 2014.

1

ATHANASIUS (c. 295–373)

LIFE

Alexandria has been called the crossroads of the ancient world. A cosmopolitan city, it was at the centre of ideas and commerce, the main centre for trade between the Roman Empire and Africa and Asia, with access to the Mediterranean and the Nile. By routing goods via the Nile to Thebes and then overland by road to the lower Red Sea, Arab middlemen could be avoided and direct access to India gained. If the Nile missed its annual overflow, there would be problems for crops. In this respect, Rome depended on Alexandria. In 355 Athanasius was accused of delaying shipment of corn to Constantinople, a serious charge in the terms of the time.

Intellectually, Alexandria was an important centre. The Jewish scholar Philo (c. 20 BC–c. 50 AD), and the Christian theologian Origen (c. 185–c. 254), were based there. Platonism was prevalent. Alexandria was the religious capital of Egypt. The bishop appointed all other Egyptian bishops and had absolute authority over them. Christianity was an urban religion at the time. By 300 approximately half of the Egyptian population was Christian. Inland, the threat to Christianity came from native Egyptian religion not from Hellenism. There was a lingering dispute over those who lapsed during the Diocletian persecution. Miletus, a rigourist, had not wanted them to be received back into the church. Monks in Upper Egypt had withdrawn from church life. The Coptic church was Coptic speaking, in contrast to the Greek speaking church in the coastal area. It was more simple and rigourist but at this point not a threat to the unity of the Egyptian church.

Athanasius was born in around 295 and had a restricted formal education. His life was packed full of action and intrigue. If it was made the subject of a movie it would be dismissed as too far-fetched. He came to the attention of the bishop, was made a deacon and accompanied bishop Alexander to Nicaea in 325, where the views of the presbyter Arius were condemned as heretical. On the death of Alexander, he was elected bishop in 328 in an election contested by the Arians. His episcopal authority was soon challenged by the large numbers of Melitian clergy. Melitus, on his own authority, ordained new clergy to replace those who had lapsed. Arius was still a presence lurking in the background. A senior clergyman in Alexandria, he had taught that Christ was not co-eternal with the Father, but was created, and had a beginning. He was deposed by an Egyptian synod in 323 and by the Council of Nicaea in 325. Melitian groups were adamant against receiving Arius back and showing any sign of weakness in that direction. The problem for Athanasius was the language used at Nicaea and currently available was ambiguous, incapable of expressing adequately how God is one and how he is three.[1]

By 332 Arian bishops were being appointed elsewhere. Arius, in turn, signed a document that persuaded Constantine that he was

---

1   Alvyn Petterson, *Athanasius* (London: Geoffrey Chapman, 1995), 9.

orthodox, although it avoided the term *homoousios*, introduced at Nicaea to assert the Son's identity of being with the Father, to which Arius objected. Constantine requested Athanasius to receive Arius back into communion, but he refused to do so. Additionally, Nicaea required there to be a gradual reconciliation with the Melitians but Athanasius had not progressed towards that. Problems were knocking at the door.

In 334 charges were made against Athanasius. First, it was alleged that he had raised a tax on linen garments—a right belonging to the pagan priesthood. Second, his presbyter Macarius was charged with desecrating a Melitian church and breaking a chalice. Third, Athanasius was charged with organizing the kidnap and murder of a Melitian bishop and using his severed hand for magical purposes. On the last allegation, in a dramatic scene, Athanasius' supporters produced the bishop alive and well, his hand still connected to the rest of his body. However, the other charges proved more difficult to refute. Constantine summoned a council but Athanasius refused to attend it as he considered an impartial hearing unlikely. However, he did attend the Council of Tyre in 335 but left for Constantinople, as the council's membership was stacked heavily against him. He was deposed on disciplinary grounds. He tried to persuade the emperor to take his side but meanwhile new charges were brought against him of delaying corn shipments to Constantinople. So Athanasius was out of office and went into exile from 335–7. However, he was not replaced as bishop and the see remained vacant.

In 337 Constantine died and the empire split three ways. Constantine II recalled Athanasius and he returned to Alexandria in November 337. It was not a happy return. Opposition was at fever pitch. He was accused of embezzling corn, and the Council of Antioch reiterated his deposition early in 339. He withdrew in March to Rome, which was more sympathetic towards him. This second period of exile was longer, lasting seven years, till 346.

At Rome, Athanasius gained the support of Pope Julius (337–52). In 341 a Council at Rome cleared him of all charges and admitted him into communion as a lawful bishop. Rival theories of church authority were competing with one another and rival councils sprang up in both east and west. Eventually after his replacement in Alexandria died, the Emperor Constans (who supported Athanasius) persuaded his brother and joint Emperor Constantius to be reconciled to Athanasius and so he returned to Alexandria to a hero's welcome in October 346. What a difference this was to the previous return!

Nevertheless, from 350 the situation took another lurch downward. Constans was assassinated in that year and by 359 Constantius was the sole emperor with semi-Arians and Arians in the ascendancy supporting him. By then he had turned against Athanasius. On the night of 7–8 February, 356 troops surrounded Athanasius' church during a service and entered the building. Athanasius managed to escape out of a side door and fled to the monks of Upper Egypt. He was replaced by a pork salesman, George of Cappadocia. This third exile lasted six years, from 356–62.

George provoked opposition by favoring the Arians and was forced to withdraw in 358. However, Julian (known as the apostate as he favored paganism) became emperor in 361, and George returned to Alexandria, only to be murdered by the mob. Julian recalled Athanasius in February 362, only for him to flee to the desert again in October for a fourth period of exile.

Julian died in 363 and was replaced by Jovian, who recalled Athanasius. But Jovian died early the following year, to be replaced by Valentinian, a supporter of Nicaea but who appointed his brother Valens—an Arian—in control of the east. Valens tried to force Arian creeds on the eastern bishops. A brief fifth exile ensued for Athanasius from October 365 until February 366.

In February 366 Valens rescinded his pro-Arian edict and Athanasius returned. The last seven years of his life were uneventful. Of 46 years as a bishop 17 were in exile, with enough twists and turns for a James Bond movie.

WRITINGS

The best known of Athanasius' works are his dogmatic and apologetic treatises, his *Oratio contra Gentes* and *De incarnatione*, possibly originally a two-volume work, and the *Orationes contra Arianos*, three extended discourses, a fourth being from another hand. Another work, *De incaranatione et contra Arianos*, is not to be confused with the two earlier mentioned works of similar name.

With someone of his stature, and given the practices of the time, it is no wonder that there are several documents that purport to be from Athanasius but are instead authored by some other unknown writer. Into this category are two volumes written against the Apollinarians, and the famous Athanasian creed.

Athanasius wrote some polemical books—the *Apologia contra Arianos* and a history of the Arians. There are a range of sermons, although most purporting to be by Athanasius are recognized as spurious. We have a few fragments of commentaries—on the Psalms, on Ecclesiastes and the Song of Solomon, and a few isolated fragments on Genesis. He wrote some ascetic treatises—a life of St. Anthony, one on virginity and so on. Then there are his Letters—(i) Festal letters, especially number 39 (367 AD) on the biblical canon providing a list that is identical with the Codex Vaticanus, stating that the deutero-canonical literature (the apocrypha) is useful for the edification of new converts but is not part of the biblical canon; (ii) synodical letters including *Ad Antiochenos*; (iii) encyclical letters; and (iv) dogmatic and pastoral letters, including *Ad Serapion* on the Holy Spirit— probably the first extended discussion of the Spirit, and *Ad Epictetus* concerning the relation between the historical Christ and the eternal Son.

THOUGHT

Incarnation

The treatise, *De incarnatione*, is a masterpiece. Some have thought Athanasius wrote it in his early twenties, around 318, when the Arian crisis erupted. However, the consensus suggests it came later, possibly in the 330s. It is a fourth century counterpart of Anselm's *Cur Deus homo?* (1098). In it Athanasius unfolds the purpose, necessity and truth of the incarnation. There are several English translations in print, including one in the Nicene and Post-Nicene Fathers set and another by Sister Penelope Lawson, a nun who was a friend of C.S. Lewis.

A number of features stand out in Athanasius' presentation.

The first matter to note is the close link he makes between creation and redemption.

> It is, then, proper for us to begin the treatment of this subject by speaking of the creation of the universe, and of God its artificer, that so it may be duly perceived that the renewal of creation has been the work of the self-same Word that made it at the beginning. For it will appear not inconsonant for the Father to have wrought its salvation in Him by whose means he made it.[2]

Note that Athanasius considers salvation in Christ to be the equivalent of the renewal of creation. This is a striking difference from conservative Protestantism, where the focus has been the deliverance of the individual from sin and where corporate elements have been present they have usually been restricted to the church.

He follows this up in a number of ways. He has *a trinitarian view of creation*, one in which the Word, Jesus Christ our Lord, was the agent in making all things out of nothing.[3] This extends

---

2   Athanasius, *On the Incarnation*, 1; see also Ibid., 14.
3   Athanasius, *Incarnation*, 3.

to providence as well for the Father through the Word orders all things, and all things are moved by him, and in him are quickened.[4] In turn, *man was created in Christ*. Since Christ *is* the image of God, and man was created *in* the image of God, man was made in Christ.

> He did not barely create man...but made them after his own image, giving them a portion even of the power of his own Word; so that having as it were a kind of reflection of the Word, and being made rational, they might be able to abide ever in blessedness, living the true life which belongs to the saints in paradise.[5]

Athanasius goes on to say 'he did not leave them destitute of the knowledge of himself', for 'he gives them a share in his own image' so that they might be able to get an idea of the Father, by such grace perceiving the image—the Word of the Father—and knowing their maker, so living a happy and truly blessed life. God made us out of nothing but also 'gave us freely, by the grace of the Word, a life in correspondence with God.'[6] If the first humans had remained good they would 'by the grace following from partaking of the Word...have escaped their natural state.'[7] Note how Athanasius has brought together creation, providence, the trinity, man, Christ and salvation into an integrated whole.

That, of course, was not the whole story for sin entered and death gained a legal hold over us that is impossible to evade.[8] We could not regain the former position by repentance alone, for that could not be sufficient to guard the just claim of God.[9] The

---

4 Athanasius, *Incarnation*, 1. Cf. Ibid., 12 where he states that the Word by his own providence makes known the Father to all so that through him they might know God.

5 Athanasius, *Incarnation*, 11.

6 Athanasius, *Incarnation*, 11.

7 Athanasius, *Incarnation*, 5.

8 Athanasius, *Incarnation*, 6.

9 Athanasius, *Incarnation*, 7.

problem was that corruption had gained a hold and man was deprived of the grace he had being in the image of God. What was required for such grace to be recalled was the Word of God who had also at the beginning made all out of nothing.

> For him it was once more both to bring the corruptible to incorruption, and to maintain intact the just claim of the Father upon all. For being the Word of the Father, and above all, he alone of natural fitness was both able to recreate everything, and worthy to suffer on behalf of all and to be ambassador for all with the Father.[10]

Again, salvation is the recreation of everything.

Athanasius moves on to explain the purpose of the incarnation.[11] The Word was not far from us before 'for no part of creation is left void of him: he has filled all things everywhere, remaining present with his own Father.' In becoming incarnate 'he takes unto himself a body, and that of no different sort from ours.'

> And thus taking from our bodies one of like nature, because all were under penalty of the corruption of death he gave it over to death in the stead of all, and offered it to the Father...to the end that, firstly, all being held to have died in him, the law involving the ruin of men might be undone (inasmuch as its power was fully spent in the Lord's body, and had no longer holding-ground against men, his peers) and that, secondly, whereas men had turned toward corruption, he might turn them again toward incorruption, and quicken them from death by the appropriation of his body and by the grace of the resurrection, banishing death from them like straw from the fire.[12]

Calvin was to echo this is his *Institute* 2:12:3.

Since it was impossible for the Word as Word to suffer death 'to this end he takes to himself a body capable of death.' So, by

---

10   Athanasius, *Incarnation*, 7.

11   Athanasius, *Incarnation*, 8.

12   Athanasius, *Incarnation*, 8.

offering to death the body he had taken, he put away death from all his peers by the offering of an equivalent. For being over all the Word by offering his own temple and corporeal instrument for the life of all satisfied the debt by his death and thus he, the incorruptible Son of God, being conjoined with all by a like nature, naturally clothed all with incorruption by the promise of his resurrection.[13] So the renewal of what was in God's image was by the presence of the very image of God, our Lord Jesus Christ.[14]

The incarnate Christ was not circumscribed in the body nor, while present in the body was he absent elsewhere, nor while he moved the body was the universe left void of his working and providence

> but, thing most marvellous, Word as he was, so far from being contained by anything, he rather contained all things himself... thus, even while present in a human body and himself quickening it, he was, without inconsistency, quickening the universe as well, and was in every process of nature, and was outside the whole, and while known from the body by his works, he was none the less manifest from the working of the universe as well.[15]

He was not bound to his body but himself wielded it so he was not only in it but also in everything and, while external to the universe, abode in his Father only.[16] This is the Catholic teaching that the person of the incarnate Christ was and is not confined to the humanity he had assumed but remains transcendent. Later, in post-Reformation disputes Lutherans were to call it the extra-Calvinisticum.

13 Athanasius, *Incarnation*, 9.
14 Athanasius, *Incarnation*, 13.
15 Athanasius, *Incarnation*, 17.
16 Athanasius, *Incarnation*, 17.

The deity of Christ

This is the issue for which Athanasius is most noted in the popular imagination. For many years his was almost a lone voice in the battle against Arianism. Arius, a presbyter at Alexandria developed a large following popularizing his teaching with a range of catchy choruses. He argued that the Son was not co-eternal with the Father and was less than equal in being and status. In fact, he was the first of God's creatures, brought forth out of nothing and not from the same substance as the Father. It gave a simple, easy rational answer to complex questions. It attacked the whole of salvation, for Jesus could not be the true revelation of God if he was merely a creature, nor could he accomplish salvation for the human race. The Council of Nicaea, called by the emperor Constantine in 325, maintained that the Son was 'of one substance with the Father.'

In the decades that followed this was the main reason for Athanasius' turbulent life. Political intrigues behind the scenes were responsible for his precarious hold on office. His *Orationes contra Arianos* contain his most rigorous theological defense of the orthodox theology of the Council of Nicaea. He marshals a range of theological and biblical arguments against the 'Ariomaniacs' as he calls them. Additionally, the first two of his letters to Serapion focus on the consubstantiality of the Son with the Father.

The humanity of Christ

In the last century or so scholars have questioned whether Athanasius had a significant place for a human soul in Jesus. Aloys Grillmeier follows this line when he acknowledges that later, after 362, Athanasius accepted that Jesus had a human soul but gave it no theological significance.[17] Johannes Quasten

---

17   Aloys Grillmeier S.J., *Christ in Christian Tradition: Volume One: From the Apostolic Age to Chalcedon (451)* (second, revised; John Bowden; Atlanta: John Knox Press, 1975), 308–28.

agrees with Grillmeier.[18] R.P.C. Hanson wrote of his having a 'space suit Christology', in which the relationship of the Son to the humanity was only as close as an astronaut's to his space suit.[19] A number of factors appear to point in this direction. First, Athanasius' pervasive terminology for the incarnate Christ is that of Logos taking into union a body. Second, while death was recognized at the time as involving a separation of the soul from the body, instead Athanasius talks of Christ as undergoing a separation of the Logos from the body. Third, one of his closest collaborators against the Arians was Apollinaris of Laodicea, who was condemned in 381 at the Council of Constantinople for his teaching that the Logos took the place of a human soul in Christ. This the church—both East and West—maintained was an incomplete humanity and jeopardized salvation. 'Whatever is not assumed cannot be healed' was the orthodox rejoinder, stemming from Gregory of Nazianzus. The picture looks grim. Was the great defender of the deity of Christ in reality a heretic? One point we should note—unlike Apollinaris, Athanasius never denied that Jesus had a human soul.

However, there is sufficient evidence to modify this assessment. Certainly, Athanasius does not devote much attention to the general area but that was not where the battle lines were drawn at the time. One of the passages relevant to the question is in his *Tomus ad Antiochenos*, written in 362.

> For they confessed also that the savior had not *a body without a soul* [italics mine] nor without sense or intelligence; for it was not possible, when the Lord had become man for us, that his body should be without intelligence: nor was the salvation effected in the Word himself a salvation of body only, but of soul also.[20]

18   Johannes Quasten, *Volume III: The Golden Age of Greek Patristic Literature from the Council of Nicea to the Council of Chalcedon*, in *Patrology* (Westminster, Maryland: Christian Classics, Inc, 1992), 72–76.

19   R.P.C. Hanson, *The Search for the Christian Doctrine of God: The Arian Controversy 318–381* (Edinburgh: T.&T. Clark, 1988), 448.

20   Athanasius, *To the Antiochenes*, 7.

Grillmeier reads 'lifeless body,' but this will not do. The final clause in the sentence can only with difficulty be rendered 'not of body only but of life also' and additionally reflects back on the earlier phrase. Moreover, Athanasius is making a direct rebuttal of the Arian denial of a human soul in Jesus.

A second passage of concern is in the *Orationes contra Arianos*, 3, written between 356 and 360. Quasten omits any reference to sections where Athanasius teaches that Christ's humanity was a whole one and points only to places where the death of Christ is said to involve only the Logos and the body.[21] But the third oration has plenty of material that belies this argument. For instance, Athanasius, in considering Luke 2:52—where Jesus is said to have grown in wisdom and stature, in favour with God and man—Athanasius says the Word did not advance as Word but he advanced humanly, since this is something that belongs to man.[22] So the humanity advanced in wisdom, becoming and appearing to all as the organ of wisdom for the operation and shining forth of the Godhead.[23] Thus, the advance is human but in the form of an appearing of the wisdom of the Word in human nature. The same factors apply at the time of Jesus' death, when he was troubled and wept.[24] According to Athanasius, these affections were not proper to the nature of the Word, as far as he was Word but were so to the flesh.[25] Statements like 'he wept' are proper to the body.[26] Suffering, weeping, toiling are things proper to the body. It was not the Word as Word who wept and was troubled but the Word as flesh—'and if too he besought that the cup might pass away, it was not the Godhead that was in terror, but this affection too was proper to the manhood.'

21   Quasten, *Patrology*, 72–76.
22   Athanasius, *Orations Against the Arians*, 3:52.
23   Athanasius, *Against the Arians*, 3:53.
24   Athanasius, *Against the Arians*, 3:54.
25   Athanasius, *Against the Arians*, 3:55.
26   Athanasius, *Against the Arians*, 3:56.

Athanasius also mentions the cry of dereliction. For the sake of this flesh he combined his own will with human weakness so as to make man undaunted in the face of death.[27]

A third passage is found in Athanasius' *Letter to Epictetus*, written before 372, which acquired almost canonical status and was quoted by the Council of Chalcedon (451) and throughout the Christological controversies. Quasten quotes from sections 5 and 6, concerning the descent into hell where Athanasius does not mention the departure of the soul from the body at all, but he does not refer at all to the important section 7.

> Now this did not come to pass putatively, as some have supposed: far be the thought: but the savior having in very truth become man, the salvation of the whole man was brought about. For if the Word were in the body putatively, as they say, and by putative is meant imaginary, it follows that both the salvation and the resurrection of man is apparent only...But truly our salvation is not merely apparent, nor does it extend to the body only, but the whole man, body and soul alike, has truly obtained salvation in the Word himself. That then which was born of Mary was according to the divine Scriptures human by nature, and the body of the Lord was a true one; but it was this, because it was the same as our body, for Mary was our sister inasmuch as we are all from Adam.[28]

Frequently Athanasius says that Christ took a human nature just like ours[29] and points to the common practice of Scripture to call man by the name of flesh.[30] Jesus' advance in wisdom occurred as the assumed humanity advanced in the divine wisdom.[31] As a result, since Christ's advance was for the sake of all, people then advance. This growth in wisdom is humanity's deification—not

---

27   Athanasius, *Against the Arians*, 3:57.

28   Athanasius, *To Epictetus*, 7.

29   Athanasius, *To Epictetus*, 5; Athanasius, *Incarnation*, 34; Athanasius, *Against the Arians*, 2:61.

30   Athanasius, *Against the Arians*, 3:30.

31   Athanasius, *Against the Arians*, 3:52–53.

becoming less human but more so. *According to the flesh* the Logos is ignorant—demonstrating that his humanity is genuine and that the Logos as Logos is not the unqualified subject.[32] This is integrally connected to soteriology—Christ's ignorance, fear, and thirst was so as to free people from these things by divinization. The Logos becomes man, and a man like all others, at once knowing and ignorant. Finally, Athanasius constantly reiterated the Nicene formula—the Logos having become flesh, became man—which was a rebuttal of the Arian denial of a human soul in Jesus. In the years since I gave this lecture, there has been an increasing dissent from the views of Grillmeier.[33]

Exchange in the incarnation—and deification

Protestants are accustomed to think of an exchange occurring at the cross where Christ took our sins and we receive his righteousness. For Athanasius, an exchange of a different, although related, kind took place in the incarnation. In becoming man, Christ received and assumed what is ours and, in doing so, sanctified it making it fit for fellowship with God. In turn, he imparted to humanity the grace of being partakers of the divine nature.

The Word was not impaired in receiving a body, that he should seek to receive a grace, but rather he deified that which he put on, and more than that, gave it graciously to the race of man... For it is the Father's glory that man, made and then lost, should be found again; and when dead, that he should be made alive... For whereas the powers in heaven, both angels and archangels, were ever worshipping the Lord, as they are now worshipping him in the name of Jesus, this is our grace and high exaltation,

---

32   Athanasius, *Against the Arians*, 3:46.

33   See Thomas G. Weinandy, *Athanasius: A Theological Introduction* (Aldershot: Ashgate, 2007), 91–96; Peter J. Leithart, *Athanasius* (Grand Rapids: Baker Academic, 2011), 117–46.

that even when he became man, the Son of God is worshipped
and the heavenly powers will not be astonished at seeing all of
us, who are of one body with him, introduced into their realms.[34]

> For so he is founded for our sakes, taking on him what is ours,
> that we, as incorporated and compacted, and bound together in him
> through the likeness of his flesh, may attain unto a perfect man, and
> abide immortal and incorruptible.[35]

> whatever he received he received humanly that for his sake men
> might have power against demons having become partakers of the
> divine nature and, in heaven, as delivered from corruption, might
> reign everlastingly.[36]

This exchange in the incarnation is the basis for Athanasius'
teaching on deification (*theōsis*); 'He was made man that we
might be made God'.[37] At the back of this lies New Testament
teaching such as 2 Peter 1:4 and much in the Johannine corpus.
He no more means that we cease to be human and become God
ontologically than he implies that the Word ceased to be God
and changed into man. Rather, the idea is that of union and
communion, just as the deity and humanity in Christ remain
such but are in unbreakable personal union. Thus

> For therefore did he assume the body originate and human, that
> having renewed it as its framer, he might deify it in himself, and thus
> might introduce it into the kingdom of heaven after his likeness.
> For man had not been deified if joined to a creature, or unless the
> Son were very God; nor had man been brought into the Father's
> presence, unless he had been his natural and true Word who had put
> on the body.[38]

---

34   Athanasius, *Against the Arians*, 1:42.
35   Athanasius, *Against the Arians*, 2:74.
36   Athanasius, *Against the Arians*, 3:40.
37   Athanasius, *Incarnation*, 54.
38   Athanasius, *Against the Arians*, 2:70.

Similarly he comments 'he has become man that he might deify us in himself'[39] and 'we are deified...by receiving the body of the Word himself' in the eucharist.[40]

The trinity

In his four letters to Serapion on the Holy Spirit, Athanasius deals at length with the relations between the persons of the trinity, with a particular focus on the Holy Spirit. The Son is of the identical being as the Father. Whatever the Father has, the Son has.[41] The trinity is indivisible, so wherever the Father is mentioned the Son should also be understood and—by the same token—where the Son is the Holy Spirit is in him.[42] The Spirit is never apart from the Word, the Son, a point Athanasius repeats time and time again.[43]

Moreover, as the Son has his particular property in relation to the Father, so does the Holy Spirit in relation to the Son.[44] The Son is the image of the Father, but so also the Holy Spirit is the image of the Son. Athanasius denies an obvious rejoinder that there are consequently two sons, maintaining the distinctiveness of the Holy Spirit in doing so, but the fact that he feels obliged to make such a point indicates how close he understands the relation of the Son and the Spirit to be. Indeed, the Holy Spirit has the same order and nature towards the Son as the Son has towards the Father. The Son is in the Father and the Father is in the Son and so also the Holy Spirit is in the Son and the Son is in the Holy Spirit. Thus, the Spirit cannot be divided from the Word.[45] So also the Spirit is in God the Father and from the

---

39   Athanasius, *Letters*, 60:4.

40   Athanasius, *Letters*, 61:2.

41   Athanasius, *Letters to Serapion on the Holy Spirit*, 2:5.

42   Athanasius, *Serapion*, 1:14.

43   Athanasius, *Serapion*, 1:14, 17, 20, 31, 3:5.

44   Athanasius, *Serapion*, 3:1.

45   Athanasius, *Serapion*, 1:20–21.

Father.[46] As the Son comes in the name of the Father, so the Holy Spirit comes in the name of the Son.[47] There is one efficacy and action of the holy trinity, for the Father makes all things through the Word by the Holy Spirit.[48]

Similarly, the Spirit receives from the Word, while the Word gives to the Spirit and whatever the Spirit has he has from the Word.[49] The Spirit is given through [the saviour] to those who believe, while whatever the Word has by nature in the Father he wishes to be given us through the Spirit irrevocably.[50] Nothing could be clearer than the intimate, unbreakable relation between the Son and the Holy Spirit in Athanasius' thought. The three persons indwell one another, are in each other. This applies as much to the Son and the Spirit as to the Son and the Father or the Father and the Spirit.

The atonement

Hanson considered that Athanasius paid little attention to the atonement. In view of his focus on theōsis he considered salvation to consist primarily in the inner transformation brought about by the incarnation and the resulting transformation by the Holy Spirit. He categorized this as salvation by a kind of sacred blood transfusion that almost does away with a doctrine of the atonement, arguing that Athanasius could not provide coherent reasons as to why Christ had to die.[51] However, as Leithart establishes, this is to miss the point that Athanasius has a great deal to say about the cross. He considers it in terms of liturgical categories, offering his body to the Father and so overcoming

46   Athanasius, *Serapion*, 1:25.

47   Athanasius, *Serapion*, 1:20.

48   Athanasius, *Serapion*, 1:20, 28, 30.

49   Athanasius, *Against the Arians*, 3:24.

50   Athanasius, *Against the Arians*, 3:25. See also Athanasius, *Against the Arians*, 3:44.

51   Hanson, *Search*, 450–51.

death, so seizing humanity and enticing it to heaven to the true worship of the Father. He also stresses the idea that Christ paid the debt which humans owed to God of death, thus releasing us from corruption and death itself.[52]

EVALUATION

Overall, the matter for which Athanasius is most famous is the one in which his most lasting contribution was made. This was the defence of the faith of the church expressed at the Council of Nicaea against Arius. The doctrine of the trinity is foundational to the whole Christian faith and Athanasius was one of its most prominent exponents. He steadfastly defended the Son being of the identical being (*homoousios*) as the Father. He did not bring about the eventual resolution of the crisis of the fourth century; that was the task of the three Cappadocians—Basil the Great, his brother Gregory of Nyssa, and Gregory of Nazianzus. However, his contribution to the end product expressed at the Council of Constantinople cannot be over estimated.

FOR FURTHER READING

Anatolios, Khaled. *Athanasius: The Coherence of his Thought.* London: Routledge, 1998.

Grillmeier, Aloys. *Christ in Christian Tradition: Volume 1.* Atlanta: Westminster Press, 1975.

Leithart, Peter J. *Athanasius.* Grand Rapids: Baker Academic, 2011.

Pettersen, Alvyn. *Athanasius.* London: Geoffrey Chapman, 1995.

Quasten, Johannes. Patrology: Volume III; *The Golden Age of*

---

52   Leithart, *Athanasius,* 154–56.

Greek Patristic Literature from the Council of Nicea to the Council of Chalcedon. Westminster, Maryland: Christian Classics, Inc., 1992.

Schaff, Phillip, ed. *Nicene and Post-Nicene Fathers of the Christian Church: Second Series, Volume IV.* Grand Rapids: Eerdmans, rpr, 1980.

Weinandy, Thomas G. *Athanasius: A Theological Introduction.* Aldershot: Ashgate, 2007.

2

GREGORY OF NAZIANZUS (C. 330–391)

LIFE

Gregory is called by the Eastern church 'the theologian,' a title he shares with the apostle John and no one else. He was born at Arianzus, a country estate belonging to his father, in the neighborhood of Nazianzus. The date of his birth is not known but it was probably around 330. His father, also Gregory, was a member of an obscure heretical sect but became a Christian through the influence of his wife, Nonna, and shortly afterwards was made bishop of Nazianzus. Our Gregory was born after his father was ordained, for the father frequently urged him to ordination saying 'You have not been so long in life as I have spent in sacrifice'—a blow to the Roman arguments for the historical antiquity of celibacy.

Gregory had a wide-ranging education. At the age of 13 he and his brother, who became a doctor in the imperial court at Constantinople, were sent to Caesarea. Then he moved to

Palestinian Caesarea, to study rhetoric. At the first of the two Caesareas, Gregory met Basil, later bishop and designated the Great, who became a life-long colleague. Later, he went to study at the University at Alexandria, while Athanasius was bishop. However, there is no evidence that they ever met. Most probably, it coincided with the second of Athanasius' exiles (340–47).

For a longer time Gregory was in Athens. On the way there his ship was nearly wrecked in a ferocious storm. Gregory was in distress for he realized he had not yet been baptized and was outside the covenant of God. Afterwards he wrote a celebrated poem, in his work *De vita sua*, which included these lines

> Despairing of everything here below,
> I raised my eyes to You, my life, my breath, my light,
> My strength, my sole salvation,
> Source of my terror and affliction.
> But even so my gentle healer,
> Who always weaves good things into disasters ...
> I said, I am Yours, Lord,
> From times past, and even now,
> Accept me once again
> The child of your honored servants
> A gift of earth and sea,
> Dedicated by the prayers of my mother
> And because of these extraordinary terrors;
> Thus shall I live for you.[1]

At Athens—he was there from the age of 18 to past 30—he renewed acquaintance with Basil and they agreed to renounce all the attractions the city held and devote themselves to the church. Basil returned sooner to Cappadocia and monastic seclusion.

---

1   John A. McGuckin, *St. Gregory of Nazianzus: An Intellectual Biography* (Crestwood, New York: St Vladimir's Seminary Press, 2001), 48–52.

When Gregory went back, his parents were still alive, his father now bishop. Part of the time he spent helping his father with his episcopal duties and part in the mountains at Basil's monastic base, where prayer, meditation, study, and manual labor were the order of the day. At this time, both Basil and Gregory made an important decision to avoid interpreting Scripture by their own individual judgment but in accordance with the authority of ancient interpreters.

Probably at Christmas 361 Gregory was ordained, against his will but with the acclamation of the people of Nazianzus. Oppressed by what he called this 'tyranny,' he fled to Pontus. However, he relented and returned to his post by Easter 362. When he preached his first sermon many stayed away in apparent protest at his actions. Later he composed an apology (defense) of his flight, saying he shrank from the huge responsibilities thrust upon him against his will.

In 370 Basil was elected bishop of Caesarea, a larger, metropolitan diocese. However, the emperor Valens was an Arian, opposed to Basil's increasing influence, supported as he was by his subordinate bishops in Cappadocia. So Valens cut Basil's diocese in half! However, as R.P.C. Hanson, himself an erstwhile bishop, says, tearing a bishop from his diocese is like trying to prize a dog from a bone.[2] Basil's response was to double the number of bishops under his jurisdiction! This included finding something for Gregory. The something was a tiny obscure backwater called Sasima, at a road junction, without water or grass, full of dust, noise and vagabonds. Gregory was furious. In fact, due to military occupation, he almost certainly never took charge. His father required his assistance at Nazianzus. After his parents' death in 374 he went into seclusion for the rest of his life, except for a short spell in Constantinople. Called there by

---

2   R. P. C. Hanson, *The Search for the Christian Doctrine of God: The Arian Controversy 318–381* (Edinburgh: T.&T. Clark, 1988), 682.

a council of bishops to promote the pro-Nicene case in advance of the arrival of the Emperor Theodosius, he devoted himself to a programme of lectures on trinitarian themes in order to expose and refute the Arians. Eventually he was consecrated as Archbishop of Constantinople, presiding briefly at the Council that resolved the trinitarian controversy. Sadly, he was altogether lacking in political and administrative skills and his leadership of the Council was inept. In the face of increasing chaos and opposition, he peremptorily resigned as president of the Council and as Archbishop. So powerful was his oratory—he was one of the greatest preachers in the history of the church—that his resignation speech was greeted by a standing ovation from an audience that was by no means favourably disposed towards him. While at Constantinople he survived an assassination attempt.[3] Jerome, translator of the Vulgate, was there at the time and greatly appreciated his preaching and learning, calling him 'my teacher in exegesis.'[4]

Gregory died in 390 or 391, around the time that Augustine was ordained bishop of Hippo. Contemporaries described him as of medium height, pale, with thick hair and a short beard, and conspicuous eyebrows. He had a scar on his right eye. His knees were worn out by excessive kneeling. His asceticism was considered overdone. He was cut off from the world and lacked experience of human nature. His love of solitude prevented him from producing the theological output he could have done. What he did write stands any test.

THOUGHT

In his time at Constantinople Gregory's main theme was worship of the trinity. Between 379 and 381 he preached five sermons

3   McGuckin, *St. Gregory of Nazianzus*, 259.
4   McGuckin, *St. Gregory of Nazianzus*, 264–5.

(the *Theological Orations*) that permanently established his reputation. As one critic put it 'Critics have rivalled each other in the praises they have heaped upon them, but no praise is so high as that of the many theologians who have found in them their own best thoughts.'[5] As McGuckin comments, they are 'the most important texts in Christian history for establishing the cardinal doctrine of the trinity.'[6]

Gregory's principal opponents were the Eunomians, followers of Eunomius, and the pneumatomachians. The Eunomians were rationalists, with a strong belief in the capacities of human logic. By logic, they maintained, we are capable of comprehending God. They assumed there to be a univocal relation between the divine and human mind (an identity of meaning for both God and man). For them, the Son is absolutely unlike the Father. God is absolute being, and generation cannot be predicated of him. Because of the correspondence between the mind of God and human reasoning, generation attributable to the Son is to be understood in terms of generation as we know it on the human level. Thus, eternal generation is inconceivable. The generation of the Son must have had a beginning. Therefore, there was a time when the Son did not exist. The Son is the first to be created and is the instrument by which God created the world. The Holy Spirit is even further removed from God.

The pneumatomachians, or fighters against the Holy Spirit, held to the Nicene faith and believed that the Son was of the identical being to the Father. However, they balked at ascribing deity to the Holy Spirit. Largely, this was due to the lack of explicit reference in the Bible to the Spirit's deity. Indeed, as Gregory states in his fifth oration, there was widespread confusion about

---

5   Philip Schaff, *Select Orations of Saint Gregory Nazianzen* (vol. 7 of *A Select Library of the Nicene and Post-Nicene Fathers of the Christian Church: Second Series*; Edinburgh: T.&T. Clark, 1989), 280.

6   McGuckin, *St. Gregory of Nazianzus*, 264.

the identity of the Spirit. Some claimed he was a creature, others that the Spirit was simply the power of God, while still others thought that he was to be counted as God but were reluctant to say so openly since it would prove controversial.

Theological Orations

(1) Preliminary discourse against the Eunomians.
Gregory discusses the principles upon which discussion should proceed. Only those who practise Christian virtue should be allowed to discuss about God.

> Discussion of theology is not for everyone, I tell you, not for everyone—it is no such inexpensive or effortless pursuit. Nor, I would add, is it for every occasion, or every audience; neither are all its aspects open to inquiry. It must be reserved for certain occasions, for certain audiences, and certain limits must be observed.[7]

It is for those 'for whom it is a serious undertaking, not just another subject like any other for entertaining small-talk, after the races, the theater, songs, food, and sex' for there are those who regard theology as a suitable topic for small talk.[8] Instead, we must remove all alien elements, look at ourselves and smooth the theologian in us, 'like a statue, into beauty.'[9] Although Gregory sounds elitist—and as an aristocrat there is an element of that— he is stressing that theological understanding requires true piety.

(2) On the doctrine of God.
Here Gregory opposes the Eunomian rationalism and establishes the limits of human knowledge.

---

7   Frederick Williams, *St. Gregory of Nazianzus: On God and Christ* (Crestwood, New York: St. Vladimir's Seminary Press, 2002), Oration 27:2, 26–7.

8   Williams, *Gregory*, Oration 27:3, 27.

9   Williams, *Gregory*, Oration 27:7, 30.

It is impossible for anyone fully to grasp the nature of God. We can only speak in negatives. 'To know God is hard, to describe him impossible.'[10] To comprehend such a great subject is quite impossible and impracticable. It is one thing to be persuaded of the existence of God and quite another to know what he is. On the other hand, God has revealed himself to humanity, to Abraham, Manoah, Isaiah and Paul. This is true knowledge but it is not direct knowledge of God's essence (from *esse*, to be).[11] They do not define God as such but are properties of the persons. Our bodily existence prevents us grasping incorporeal realities. This inability to know the essence of God is designed to keep us from pride, to increase our valuation of the knowledge of God, and to sustain us in the trials of life by directing us to its attainment in the hereafter as a reward for faithful service now.

(3) On the Son.

Gregory proceeds to unfold his own teaching, remarking on the ease with which one can criticize others while failing to advance anything constructive oneself.

> To censure...is a trivial task—anyone so minded can do it quite easily. But to substitute one's own view takes a man of true religion and sound sense.[12]

He starts by affirming the monarchy (the principle of unity in God). The Cappadocians have been—wrongly—taken to task by some for making the Father the cause of the deity of the Son and the Holy Spirit, by arguing that the Father is the source of the divine essence. Nothing could be further from Gregory's mind. The monarchy is not limited to one person so that, although the persons are numerically distinct there is no severance of essence.

---

10   Williams, *Gregory*, Oration 28:4, 39.
11   Williams, *Gregory*, Oration 28:21, 52–3.
12   Williams, *Gregory*, Oration 29:1, 69.

The Father is the begetter and emitter, the Son is the begotten, and the Holy Spirit the emission, but this is so in the context of equality of nature, a union of mind, an identity of motion.[13] Where Gregory considers the Father to be the source of the Son and the Spirit, he is referring to the relations between the three, not to the indivisible divine essence.[14] The begetting of the Son occurred when the Father was not begotten, and the procession of the Spirit took place when the Son was begotten and not proceeding, beyond time and above reason, for there never was when the Father was not, nor was there such with respect to the Son and the Holy Spirit. The Son and the Spirit are from the Father but not after the Father.[15] To be begotten and to proceed are concurrent with to be.[16] All this is, of course, beyond our comprehension. Yet this does not negate it, any more than we reject God's existence because we cannot comprehend him.[17] The begetting of the Son by the Father establishes their identity of nature, for the offspring is of the same nature as the parent.[18]

Gregory continues to maintain the incomprehensibility of God's essence against Eunomian rationalism. Perhaps at some point in the future we may know 'in the time to come, when we are free of this dense gloom.'[19] The thing to note, he says, is that the distinction of Father and Son is outside the essence, for begetting and being begotten (and, we may add by inference, procession) is a property of the persons (the hypostases), not the

---

13   Williams, *Gregory*, Oration 29:2, 70.
14   See Williams, *Gregory*, Oration 30:7, 9–99; T.A. Noble, 'Paradox in Gregory Nazianzen's Doctrine of the Trinity,' *Studia Patristica* XXVII (1993): 9–99.
15   Williams, *Gregory*, Oration 29:3, 71.
16   Williams, *Gregory*, Oration 29:9, 76–7.
17   Williams, *Gregory*, Oration 29:28, 69–70.
18   Williams, *Gregory*, Oration 29:10, 78.
19   Williams, *Gregory*, Oration 29:11, 79.

one essence.[20] They do not define God as such but are properties of the persons. In the same way, Father does not denote the essence of God but 'the manner of being, which holds good between the Father and the Son,' which also denotes the identity of nature between the Father who begets and the Son who is begotten.[21] The Son is called Son to denote this identity of nature, as well as because he is of the Father in terms of *relatio*.[22] Thus, there was never a time when the Father was without the Son, nor the Son without the Father.[23] Since his opponents were accustomed to cite biblical passages attributing weakness and subordination to the Son, Gregory points to the incarnation as the occasion for such descriptions. 'You must predicate the more sublime expressions of the Godhead…and the lowlier ones of…him who…became incarnate.'[24] He remained God while adding human nature,[25] while his humanity was united to God and became one person so that we might be made God to the same extent that he was made man. Gregory concludes with a shot across the bows of the rationalists.'When we abandon faith to take the power of reason as our shield…then reason gives way in the face of the vastness of the realities…Thus it is that, as Paul too judges, smartness of argument is revealed as a nullifying of the Cross. Faith, in fact, is what gives fullness to our reasoning.'[26]

(4) On the Son.
In the fourth oration Gregory continues to answer the charges that the Bible refers to the Son as weak and subordinate. Many times Scripture refers to Christ fulfilling the Father's will. In

20   Williams, *Gregory*, Oration 29:12, 80.
21   Williams, *Gregory*, Oration 29:16, 84.
22   Williams, *Gregory*, Oration 30:20, 109–10.
23   Williams, *Gregory*, Oration 29:17, 85.
24   Williams, *Gregory*, Oration 29:18, 86.
25   Williams, *Gregory*, Oration 29:18, 86.
26   Williams, *Gregory*, Oration 29:21, 88–9.

this, Gregory argues, he makes our condition his own and so presents it to God.[27] These are all to be explained in terms of the incarnation and the work of salvation on our behalf.

(5) On the Holy Spirit.

Here the *pneumatomachi* (fighters against the Holy Spirit) were the problem. They were regarded as followers of Macedonius, a deposed bishop, and were also known as Macedonians, although there is no clear evidence that Macedonius held to the views that are connected with his name. They denied the deity of the Holy Spirit and placed him in a position even more removed from God than they did the Son.

> It is not just that men exhausted by discussions of the Son are more eager to take on the Spirit—they must have something to blaspheme or life would be unlivable—but also that we become worn out by the quantity of issues.[28]

Gregory's opponents were biblical fundamentalists. The Arians, Eunomians and Macedonians all appealed to the Bible and contended that the pro-Nicenes were unscriptural, since they used terms like *homoousios*, trinity and such like which were not in the Bible. 'Time and time again you repeat the argument about *not being in the Bible*,' Gregory complains. He points out that the fathers, in their handling of the Bible, had penetrated to its inner meaning.[29] Instead, the heretics' 'love for the letter is but a cloak for irreligion.'[30] Scripture uses metaphors and figures of speech. Slavery to a literal interpretation is an erroneous exegetical and theological method. In fact, the heretics favorite terms for God, 'unbegotten' and 'unoriginate' are not in the Bible at all![31]

---

27 Williams, *Gregory*, Oration 30:5, 96.
28 Williams, *Gregory*, Oration 31:2, 117.
29 Williams, *Gregory*, Oration 31:21, 133.
30 Williams, *Gregory*, Oration 31:3, 118.
31 Williams, *Gregory*, Oration 31:22–24, 133–6.

Gregory uses the commonly accepted theology of deification to make a point. In salvation we are made God. But if the Holy Spirit is not from eternity, how can he make me God, or join me with the Godhead?[32] Gregory points to the confusion that currently existed over the status of the Spirit:

> Amongst our own experts some took the Holy Spirit as an active process, some as a creature, some as God. Others were agnostic on this point *out of reverence,* as they put it, *for Scripture, which has given no clear revelation either way.* On these grounds they offer him neither worship nor disrespect; they take up a sort of halfway (or should I say 'a thoroughly pitiful'?) position about him.[33]

His opponents were asking Gregory to make clear definitions, since they supposed human logic capable of unfolding the truth about God. He responds by saying that with respect to the procession of the Spirit, as with the begetting of the Son, human language about God is not to be understood in a univocal sense,[34] so that to define the procession of the Spirit and the generation of the Son is beyond us:

> What then is 'proceeding'? You explain the ingeneracy of the Father, and I will give you a biological account of the Son's begetting and the Spirit's proceeding—and let us go mad the pair of us for prying into God's secrets.[35]

How, then, does the Spirit differ from the Son? The difference of manifestation or relations has given the different names. Their respective properties (unbegotten, begotten, proceeding) has given them their respective names (Father, Son, Holy Spirit) so as 'to safeguard the distinctness of the three hypostases within the sin-

---

32 Williams, *Gregory*, Oration 31:4, 119.
33 Williams, *Gregory*, Oration 31:5, 119–20.
34 Williams, *Gregory*, Oration 31:7, 121–2.
35 Williams, *Gregory*, Oration 31:8, 122.

gle nature and quality of the Godhead.'[36] So Gregory announces his epoch-making breakthrough; '*What then? Is the Spirit God?* Certainly. *Is he consubstantial?* Yes, if he is God.'[37] McGuckin calls this simple statement 'a thunderclap in its historical context...a new epoch in the history of Nicene theology.'[38]

Appropriately, Gregory turns to a consideration of worship. The Spirit is the one in whom we worship and in whom we pray. Thus, prayer to the Spirit is, in effect, the Spirit offering prayer or adoration to himself. Worship of the one is worship of the three, due to the one indivisible being of God.[39] He adds

> We have one God because there is a single Godhead. Though there are three objects of belief, they derive from the single whole and have reference to it. They do not have degrees of being God or degrees of priority over against one another. They are not sundered in will or divided in power...the Godhead exists undivided in things divided...When we look at the Godhead, the primal cause, the sole sovereignty, we have a mental picture of the single whole, certainly. But when we look at the three in whom the Godhead exists...we have three objects of worship.'[40]

There follows a major innovation. Gregory explains the comparative reticence of Scripture on the Holy Spirit by the historical and progressive outworking of revelation. The OT proclaimed the Father openly, and the Son more obscurely. The NT made known the Son, and suggested the deity of the Spirit. Now the Spirit himself dwells among us, so that we have been given a clearer manifestation of himself. 'It was dangerous, too, for the Holy Spirit to be made...an extra burden, when the Son had not been received.'[41] Now, worship and baptism establish the Spirit's

---

36   Williams, *Gregory*, Oration 31:10, 123.

37   Williams, *Gregory*, Oration 31:10, 123.

38   McGuckin, *St. Gregory of Nazianzus*, 305.

39   Williams, *Gregory*, Oration 31:12, 125–6.

40   Williams, *Gregory*, Oration 31:14, 127–8.

41   Williams, *Gregory*, Oration 31:26, 137.

deity for 'were the Spirit not to be worshipped, how could he deify me through baptism? If he is to be worshipped, why not adored? And if to be adored, how can he fail to be God?'[42] In short, if the Spirit were not God, salvation itself would unravel, as only one who is God could so transform us. For Gregory, the trinity is not an abstract puzzle but the heart of the Christian faith and the centre of true worship. 'But when I say God, I mean Father, Son, and Holy Spirit.'[43]

We conclude with a passage Calvin, in his *Institute*, said 'vastly delights me.' As we reflect on it, perhaps we can see why.

> This I give you to share, and to defend all your life, the one Godhead and power, found in the three in unity, and comprising the three separately; not unequal, in substances or natures, neither increased nor diminished by superiorities or inferiorities; in every respect equal, in every respect the same; just as the beauty and the greatness of the heavens is one; the infinite conjunction of three infinite ones, each God when considered in himself; as the Father, so the Son; as the Son so the Holy Spirit; the three one God when contemplated together; each God because consubstantial; one God because of the monarchia. No sooner do I conceive of the one than I am illumined by the splendour of the three; no sooner do I distinguish them than I am carried back to the one. When I think of any one of the three I think of him as the whole, and my eyes are filled, and the greater part of what I am thinking escapes me. I cannot grasp the greatness of that one so as to attribute a greater greatness to the rest. When I contemplate the three together, I see but one torch, and cannot divide or measure out the undivided light.[44]

FOR FURTHER READING

McGuckin, John A. *St. Gregory of Nazianzus: An Intellectual Biography.* Crestwood, New York: St Vladimir's Seminary Press, 2001.

42   Williams, *Gregory*, Oration 31:28, 139.
43   Gregory Nazianzen, Oration 38 *on the Theophany, or Birthday of Christ*, 8.
44   Gregory Nazianzen, Oration 40 *on Holy Baptism*, 41.

Noble, T.A. 'Paradox in Gregory Nazianzen's Doctrine of the
       Trinity.' *Studia Patristica* XXVII (1993): 94–99.

Schaff, Philip. Select Orations of Saint Gregory Nazianzen.
       Vol. 7 of *A Select Library of the Nicene and Post-Nicene
       Fathers of the Christian Church: Second Series.* Edinburgh:
       T.&T. Clark, 1989. See particularly the Five Theological
       Orations, Oration 38 on the Theophany, or Birthday of
       Christ, and Oration 40 on Holy Baptism.

Williams, Frederick. *St. Gregory of Nazianzus: On God and
       Christ.* Crestwood, New York: St. Vladimir's Seminary
       Press, 2002. This includes a translation of the Five
       Theological Orations.

3

AUGUSTINE (354–430)

LIFE

Augustine was born in 354 at Thagaste in North Africa, an area in present-day Algeria. His father became a believer shortly before his death in 372. His mother, Monica, was a devout Christian and at the same time ambitious for Augustine's success. His education at Carthage was based on classical Latin literature and centred in rhetoric. At that time, mastery of public speech was essential for success in law or public service. As a result, Augustine became highly skilled in literary expression. However, he failed to master Greek—although he knew far more than he has sometimes been credited—and was not familiar with Hebrew.

Augustine was a catechumen from infancy, a candidate under preparation for baptism. Infant baptism was not universally practised at the time. However, despite his upbringing, his critical and enquiring mind was not satisfied with Christianity and his allegiance to the church was undermined by contact with

Manichaeism. This sect held to a radical form of dualism, maintaining that there were two co-equal principles in the cosmos, good and evil.

Manichaeism was founded by Mani in Mesopotamia, who was executed in 276. Mani claimed a revelation from God. His followers believed that theirs was a universal religion transcending all others. They proposed a solution to the problem of evil. In an attempt to protect God from contact with evil, they propounded an extreme form of ontological dualism. There were two co-equal, co-eternal kingdoms, a kingdom of light (good), and a kingdom of darkness (evil). Good was passive and invaded by evil. In tandem with this, they radically opposed body and soul, being extreme ascetics. They rejected the authority of the church and also the OT.

Augustine became a Manichaeian auditor for ten years, at first proselytizing enthusiastically but gradually growing disillusioned with the movement. His disillusionment with the Manichees was largely due to its leaders' lack of education and the inconsistencies in their teachings. He came to see it as essentially static and as by-passing the quest for truth that classical philosophy had made its concern.

During this time he taught rhetoric at Thagaste (375–6), and later at Carthage (376–83), after which he went to Rome to further his career. He moved to Milan the following year as professor of rhetoric. Meanwhile he spent time with an entourage of fellow philosophers and intellectuals, accompanied by his mother, who had followed him from Africa and persistently prayed for his conversion. He had also acquired a concubine, with whom he produced a son, Adeodatus (given by God).

In Milan Augustine came into contact with the bishop, Ambrose. At first he was simply impressed by Ambrose's eloquence. Ambrose had been influenced by *neo-Platonism.* As a result Augustine was introduced to neo-Platonist writings by Plotinus and Porphyry. This helped his emancipation from Manichaeism. It led him to view God as a transcendental immaterial being and, importantly, to view evil not as a positive ontological reality but as something negative, as a privation of goodness. This released him from the two correlative kingdoms of the Manichees. He was now open to Christianity as he had not been before.

In the summer of 386 he was in a Milan garden when he heard a small child singing repeatedly, 'tolle, lege' (pick up and read). He picked up a scroll of Scripture, and opened it and began to read from Romans 13:13–14, words that were eventually to shape the history of the western world.

> ...not in orgies and drunkenness, not in sexual immorality and sensuality, not in quarrelling and jealousy. But put on the Lord Jesus Christ, and make no provision for the flesh, to gratify its desires.[1]

Augustine abandoned his philosophical career and went into retreat with friends and his mother in order to pursue the quest for wisdom unhindered by other preoccupations. He saw himself as a Christian philosopher at this point, a Catholic neo-Platonist, with a philosophy that made allowance for progress and creative intellectual development. At the same time, told by Ambrose to read Isaiah in preparation for baptism, he was unable to understand it! He was baptized by Ambrose at Easter 387. He continued to lead a life of creative leisure, his small circle in a state of perpetual intellectual excitement. Augustine sent his concubine back to Africa to fend for herself, sadly a not uncommon feature of the time, and later in 387 his mother died. The following year he made the return journey to Thagaste, forming a community of servants of God, dedicated laymen in a quasi-monastic setting. Shortly afterwards, compounding his grief, his son also died.

---

1   See Gerald Bonner, *St. Augustine of Hippo: Life and Controversies* (Norwich: Canterbury Press, 1986), 91; Peter Brown, *Augustine of Hippo: A Biography* (London: Faber and Faber, 1967), 108–9.

A watershed occurred in 391. Visiting the seaport of Hippo to gain a servant for his community, Augustine was forced by popular acclaim into the priesthood, driven to the front of the church by the people, who were shouting loudly. The catholic church needed an articulate spokesman at Hippo due to the threat from the Donatists, who had separated from the church due to its perceived impurity and compromises. Four years later he was made bishop, despite there being a bishop already and in the face of the prohibition of the Council of Nicaea (325) on multiple bishops in any one see. His community moved from Thagaste to Hippo to join him. From 391 he abandoned neo-Platonism. Thereafter his life was devoted to the church and to his writings. He died in 430 at the age of 76, as the barbarians were in the process of wiping out Roman civilization in North Africa. Augustine's work was soon destroyed in the land of his birth but his greatest legacy was to reach down the centuries throughout the Western church.

THOUGHT AND MAJOR WRITINGS

The Donatist controversy

The Donatists were spreading rapidly in North Africa. They stressed the holiness of the church, and had a negative attitude to the State. They stressed separation from sin to the extent that sinners had no part in the church. Unworthy bishops should be removed. The Catholics, for their part, had a prime emphasis on the unity of the church. They believed the church could absorb the world and retain its identity. The Donatists wanted separation from society, while the Catholics wanted to dominate and absorb it. Donatism had begun earlier in the fourth century when Caecilian became bishop of Carthage. He had been ordained by a *traditor* (one who had handed over sacred books during a time of persecution). Eighty bishops declared Caecilian's ordination invalid and elected Donatus bishop instead. The Emperor Constantine supported Caecilian since he wanted a united church and Caecilian was the existing bishop. The question surrounded the relationship between the unity of the church and its holiness. It is an issue that surfaces repeatedly down the years.

Over the course of time, Augustine produced a number of anti-Donatist writings, such as *On Baptism, against the Donatists* and *The Correction of the Donatists.* He emphasized the mystery of predestination, seeing the church and the world as two overlapping, but not identical, circles. Some who were not part of the church might still be among the elect, while some who were in the church might prove not to be elect. The church will not be pure as long as this world lasts. Only at the day of judgement will the tares finally be separated from the wheat.

On the other hand, no one could be pure and holy while separated from the body of Christ. Thus, there is in the Catholic church something that is not Catholic, while there is something Catholic outside the Catholic church. But since complete purity is not attainable in this life there is no excuse for schism. At the same time, the church must strive for purity. The holiness of the church is not the holiness of its clergy or its members but the holiness of the grace dispensed in the sacraments. It is objective.

The unity of the church is also a necessary corollary of God's grace, for there is one baptism, one church, one faith. The sin that threatens the church is not adultery or individual apostasy but schism. The conflict is between sacramental grace and perfectionism. Augustine's view became the normative view of Western Christianity.

The City of God

This massive and justly renowned treatise was written from 412–25. It was occasioned by the sack of Rome in 410 by Alaric. It is hard to overestimate the impact of this event. It was an incredible shock for the Romans. The city at the heart of the

Empire that had dominated the world for centuries was invaded and pillaged by barbarians. Its impact was akin to the events of 9/11 on the United States. Past Roman successes had been seen as the result of civic virtues, which set them apart from the Greeks and the Barbarians. These virtues were dependent on the Roman gods. Christianity, with its growing strength, endangered the Roman state since the gods were enraged at the mass transfer of allegiance to the church. Each nation and ethnic group had its own deities. If these gods were happy the Empire would prosper. The problem with Christianity, in the eyes of pagans, was that it was international and so undermined the whole gamut of religions in the Roman world, especially those to which the Romans themselves were attached. The sack of Rome was the Christians' fault. Particularly, the removal of the pagan altar from the Senate in 382, when the emperor Theodosius made Christianity the official religion, was to blame.

At the same time, many Christians were perplexed as to why God allowed this event to occur. Would he protect the church? In response, Augustine wrote *The City of God*. In it he argues that Christian virtues have not undermined Rome, since these are basically the same as the pagan ones. Instead, it is the pagan vices that are responsible. The first two of five parts of the whole are devoted to undermining pagan worship and its associated worldview, followed by a critical evaluation of neo-Platonism, appreciating its acknowledgement of the uniqueness of God but also exposing its neglect of God's action in history.

Augustine then proceeds to unfold a biblical understanding of history. God is the creator and has made humans to be related to him in communion. Being made in the image of God, we share in the trinity. Mankind's unity was broken after the fall, with love for God and love of self in conflict. Correspondingly, there are two cities—the city of peace, the church, and the earthly city, devoted to the love of self rather than God. Here and now they represent the city of God and the city of this world. Augustine then unfolds the historical account in the Bible. The city of God entails communion with the trinity in the course of human history. Augustine unfolds its interaction with the earthly city from Genesis onwards. In the final section he deals with the ultimate fulfillment in the resurrection and the life of the world to come.

At the heart of this work is a contrast Augustine draws between Rome and the church. Rome is marked by political power, whereas the apostles were martyred. There exists a correspondence, but not identity, with church and state. There are certain areas of co-operation between the two cities, since all desire peace rather than war. However, human beings prefer an unjust peace. Augustine appears to exclude the idea of a distinctively Christian culture in the state. Ultimately the city of God is oriented to the future and the resurrection.

The trinity

Augustine's treatise *De trinitate* dominated Western trinitarianism until the twentieth century, until Barth—but even then Barth could not escape the frame of thought Augustine bequeathed. Augustine published the treatise since a number of pirated editions were already on the market.

In writing it, he was expressing his agreement with the settlement of the trinitarian crisis that had bedevilled the church in the fourth century. This resolution had occurred at the Council of Constantinople in 381, largely due to the work of the three Cappadocians, Basil the Great, Gregory of Nyssa, and Gregory of Nazianzus.

The theme that tends to dominate many people's attention in this work is Augustine's famous series of psychological illustrations of the trinity. This is clearly an ingenious argument. However, it has a number of flaws that have bedevilled Western trinitarianism ever since due to its immense influence. The prime point is that he starts from the unity of God and so has some difficulty in according reality to the three persons. In fact, at times he sounds almost modalist. Modalism was the idea that Father, Son and Holy Spirit were merely roles played by the one God on different occasions and did not represent eternal, antecedent realities in God. They were not eternal, co-equal persons but virtually attributes. In other words, modalism was not trinitarianism. Augustine was clearly not a modalist. However, at times his psychological illustrations can give that impression. He makes very clear that he is not actually attempting to prove the doctrine of the trinity from the inner workings of the human mind. Rather, he is addressing a question from a friend, Nebridius, that had dominated his mind from early in his career. This was how one reality could be expressed in three distinct ways while being indivisible.

Moreover, most of the book is devoted to biblical exegesis. In this Augustine establishes that the Son is of the same identical being as the Father, as is the Holy Spirit. He goes on to discuss the relations between the three and how we should understand biblical passages that talk of the Son in relation to the Father. There are some passages, Augustine affirms, that concern the Son as he is God. Others describe him as less than God; these refer to his incarnation as man. There are still more passages that refer to him as the Son in relation to the Father, and so speak of him as being sent. It is striking how Augustine—as Athanasius and the Cappadocians—often refers to the Old Testament in considering the trinity. So far from being a philosophical treatise, the bulk of what Augustine writes is a consideration of the teaching of the Bible.

One particularly striking aspect of Augustine's discussion is the idea of the double procession of the Holy Spirit. The Nicene creed, composed by the assembled bishops at Constantinople in resolving the trinitarian crisis in 381 stated that the Spirit proceeds from the Father. It did not deny that the Spirit proceeded also from the Son, although that is an anachronistic matter as the claim had not yet arisen. However, the tenor of the creed—and

the debates that led up to it—was that the Father is the source
of the personal identity of both the Son and the Holy Spirit.
What Augustine argued is that, in being indivisibly one with the
Father, the Son receives all things from him, and that includes
being the spirator of the Holy Spirit. The Spirit thus proceeds
from the Father and the Son as from a common source. In later
centuries, the Latin church would introduce this into its version
of the creed, confessing that the Spirit proceeds from the Father
and the Son (*filioque*). It was to be the major point of theological
contention between the Latin and Greek churches and would
eventually bring about a rupture of relations between them.[2]

Grace and the Pelagian controversy

The sovereignty of God was crucial for Augustine. God's will
determines human actions. Predestination is a preparation for
grace, which in turn is the bestowal of the gift of salvation itself.
Augustine applied double predestination to individuals as well as
the two cities. He called it a mystery. This doctrine was severely
challenged in the Pelagian controversy.

Much of Augustine's writing on this great theme was directed
against Pelagius and his followers, particularly Julian of Eclanum.
Pelagius was a British monk based in Rome. Alarmed at the
decadence of Rome, he began to spread his views in the first
decade of the fifth century. Pelagius was not apparently intending
to stir up controversy since he was peaceable and not ambitious.
Eventually he moved to Palestine, via north Africa. His followers,
especially Julian of Eclanum, took up his ideas and spread them.

According to the Pelagians, the Bible requires perfection of
humans. This implies that after the fall humans have the ability
to obey the commands of God and to attain to sinless perfection,

---

2   Augustine, *On the Holy Trinity, Doctrinal Treatises, Moral Treatises*
(Nicene and post-Nicene fathers: first series, volume 3; Philip Schaff; Peabody,
Massachusetts: Hendrickson, 1995), 15:27–9, 47–8.

on the basis of Matthew 5:48. Since we are able to respond to the requirements of God, we are held personally responsible for any failure to do so. Thus, Pelagians had a voluntaristic view of faith; it was seen as a matter of the human will and is in the power of all people to exercise. Indeed, it was pointed out that the Bible describes people who lived perfect lives—Abel, Enoch, Joseph, John and especially the Virgin Mary. Augustine agreed with this about Mary for it seemed essential that she be preserved from sin or else Jesus would inherit original sin and salvation be jeopardized. Grace was necessary every moment of our lives but it complements nature and rewards it for doing its best. Thus the ability to believe comes from God but the willing and acting of faith depends on our free will. Grace is thus resistible. The Pelagians regarded Augustine's doctrine of original sin as absurd and unjust. Everyone is accountable for their own sins only and cannot be held responsible for the sin of Adam. The only way we are implicated in Adam's sin is by the fact that we imitate it by sinning ourselves. They saw Augustine as teaching fatalism, with humans enslaved to forces outside their control. Instead, sin is carried on by imitation not by transmission through the propagation of the race. It is an act of the human will, a matter we choose freely to do. Even when we personally sin, our will is as free as it was before. We retain the power of contrary choice, being able to choose good or evil at any point.[3]

---

3   For a detailed description of the Pelagian teachings, see Peter Brown, *Augustine of Hippo: A Biography* (London: Faber and Faber, 1967); P. Brown, 'Pelagius and His Supporters: Aims and Environment,' *JTS* 21 (1970): 56–72; Gerald Bonner, 'How Pelagian Was Pelagius?' *Studia Patristica* 9 (1966): 350–58; Gerald Bonner, *Augustine and Recent Research on Pelagius* (Villanova: Villanova University Press, 1972); Gerald Bonner, *St. Augustine of Hippo: Life and Controversies* (Norwich: Canterbury Press, 1986), 138–40; J. Ferguson, *Pelagius: A Historical and Theological Study* (Cambridge: Cambridge University Press, 1956); Matthew Levering, *The Theology of Augustine: An Introductory Guide to His Most Important Writings* (Grand Rapids: Baker Academic, 2013), 82–84; *Augustine through the Ages* (Grand Rapids, Eerdmans, 1999) 638–40.

This controversy was Augustine's severest challenge, since Pelagius, Julian and their supporters were inside the Catholic church. They were identified as Christians and had not abandoned the Christian community. It called forth the greatest volume of Augustine's polemical work. In doing so, he addressed the hugely significant issues of sin, grace and the human will. Among these treatises are *On the Spirit and the Letter, On Nature and Grace, On the Grace of Christ and Original Sin, On the Merits and Remission of Sins, On Grace and Free Will,* and *On Rebuke and Grace.*

According to Augustine, in the sin of Adam the entire race sinned, since sin is transmitted through propagation. This was not Manichaeian, for he insisted on the inherent goodness of creation. Man had a good creation but a corrupt propagation. Nature had not been destroyed but gravely wounded, and needed to be healed by God's grace.

Grace is not based on any preceding merits or human works. We could not love God unless he had first loved us. Prevenient grace (grace going before) is seen in infant baptism, proving that there is a universal need for grace, even before a person has had a chance to commit sins of his or her own. Since God is sovereign he is not bound to the church and sacraments but nevertheless he freely has chosen to bind himself to them. Thus we ourselves cannot determine who the elect are.

Augustine famously wrote: 'I should not believe the gospel except as moved by the authority of the catholic church.'[4] The authority of the church even validates the Bible although it is corrected by Scripture, whereas the Bible never needs correction. There is no contradiction between the authority of the Bible and that of the church. In appealing to the authority of the church, Augustine was highlighting the point that the church's doctrine is the distillation of its best biblical exegesis. However,

---

4   Augustine, *Against the Epistle of Manichaeus Called Fundamental,* NPNF, First series, 4:131.

his language could be understood in a number of different ways and, with the heightened power of the Papacy in later centuries this comment, and the questions underlying it, would prove to be the major source of contention between the church of Rome and Protestantism.

For Augustine grace is sovereignly determined and effected by God and yet it is also mediated, dependent on the will of God and yet obtainable through the sacraments. An unfortunate element of this was his famous definition of sacraments as outward and visible means of inward and spiritual grace. This had the effect of severing the sacraments from Christ by inserting an ontological substratum called grace between Christ and the recipients. Again, we can see the remnants of his earlier Manichaeism and neo-Platonism, both encouraging a split between the natural and physical on the one hand, and the spiritual on the other.

Thus the respective orders in salvation were as follows. For Pelagianism, human free will is the key in the response to the gospel, for after the fall people retain the ability to believe. God's grace follows and is resistible, since free will is operative throughout. Free will for the Pelagians entailed the power of contrary choice. Augustine agreed that humans are free agents, that the decisions they make are truly theirs, but argued that due to sin fallen people inevitably choose to reject God.

In contrast, Augustine maintained that God's grace comes first. Prevenient grace precedes any possible action on the part of the human being and is effective in election and baptism. In operating grace, God sets the will free, moving and acting upon it to turn it to faith and repentance. Following this, the will—now freed—acts with God's co-operating grace in the ministry of the church in Word and sacrament.

Pelagianism was condemned as heresy by the Council of Carthage in 418. While it was a controversy that occurred exclusively in the Western, Latin church, the East—at the council of Ephesus in 431—also pronounced deposition from the clergy for anyone who agreed with the theology of Celestine, probably meaning Caelestius, one of the leading Pelagians.[5] However, Pelagianism does not go away so easily. It is the default position of the sincere, religious, but unrepentant human heart. As James I. Packer described it, it is the assumption of the keen and zealous Christian who has little or no interest in doctrine and, as he argued, it was the settled position of the Keswick movement as it was historically based.[6]

LEGACY

Augustine was unrivalled for a thousand years. Even today, the theology of the Western church cannot be understood apart from Augustine. However, like all great seminal thinkers—such as Origen, Calvin, and Barth—he is claimed as the founder of a wide variety of disparate positions. Warfield commented that the Reformation was a conflict between Augustine's doctrine of the church and Augustine's doctrine of grace.[7] In that sense, the comment that the middle ages and Reformation are a series of footnotes to Augustine has more than a few grains of truth to it. His is the dominant voice on a wide range of matters central to the Christian faith—the trinity; predestination, sin and grace; the sacraments; and the relationship between church and state.

5   Henry R. Percival, *The Seven Ecumenical Councils of the Undivided Church: Their Canons and Dogmatic Decrees* (A Select Library of Nicene and Post-Nicene Fathers of the Christian Church: Second Series; Edinburgh: T.&T. Clark, 1997 reprint), 229.

6   James I. Packer, "'Keswick' and the Reformed Doctrine of Sanctification,' *EQ* 27 (1955): 153–67.

7   Benjamin B. Warfield, *Calvin and Augustine* (Repr. Philadelphia: The Presbyterian and Reformed Publ. Co., 1956), 322.

FOR FURTHER READING

A Select Library of the Nicene and Post-Nicene Fathers of the Christian Church. First Series. Rpr., Grand Rapids: Eerdmans, 1994. There are many individual works of Augustine in print in English translation and many can be found online at Christian Classics Ethereal Library, located at www.ccel.org

Allan D. Fitzgerald, ed. *Augustine through the Ages.* Grand Rapids: Eerdmans, 1999. This is a 900 page collection of essays of varying length on Augustine and his interpreters.

Gerald Bonner. *St. Augustine of Hippo: Life and Controversies.* Norwich: Canterbury Press, 1986.

Peter Brown. *Augustine of Hippo: A Biography.* London: Faber and Faber, 1967. The classic biography that also interacts with Augustine's thought and writing.

Serge Lancel. *Saint Augustine.* London: SCM, 2002. Outstanding on the socio-economic and political background to Augustine's life and ministry, especially in its north African context.

Matthew Levering. *The Theology of Augustine: An Introductory Guide to his most important works.* Grand Rapids: Baker Academic, 2013. An outstanding summary of seven of the most significant of Augustine's works.

4

CHARLES THE GREAT (741–814)

HISTORICAL CONTEXT

In 632 Mohammed had a vision at Mecca in Arabia and a militant new religion erupted on the world stage. By 642 Islam had spread throughout the Middle East, along the whole of North Africa and soon over the Mediterranean into Spain. Eventually the Moslems crossed the Pyrenees into France, threatening the whole of Europe. In 732 (exactly 100 years after its beginning) Islamic armies were defeated at Tours by the forces of Charles Martel, the Frankish king in one of the most crucial and decisive battles of European history.

Earlier, in 499, the then king of the Franks, Clovis, had become a Christian and been baptized. However, Christianity had been gravely weakend by the state of society in the wake of the collapse of the Roman empire. The church remained the one solvent institution but standards of education and life slumped drastically. Corruption, violence and incompetence characterized

Frankish society and public life. The effect on the church was severe. Few clergy had any education and literacy, without which it was possible to be an evangelist but not to sustain a teaching ministry. In fact, even where it existed, preaching was largely confined to feast days (Christmas, Easter, Pentecost).[1]

LIFE AND CHARACTER

Charles was born on 2 April 742. His father, Pepin, had succeeded his grandfather Charles Martel as king. Shortly before his death, Pepin divided the kingdom into two, to be shared between his two sons Charles and Carloman. Both were enthroned and anointed on 9 October 768. After a period of stress and tension between the two brothers, Carloman suddenly died on 4 December 771 and Charles seized his brother's share of the kingdom in a *coup d'état*.

Military conquests and imperial expansion

There followed a period of vigorous conquest by Charles until the kingdom was roughly the size of the former western Roman empire. First, came his conquest of Italy, establishing the power of his rule and effectively asserting his protection of the church and thus suzerainty over the Pope. In a decisive battle, he brought the independent Lombard kingdom to an end in 773–4.[2] He and the Pope swore oaths of mutual fidelity over the grave of St Peter. Charles' son Pepin was appointed king of Italy by the Pope in 780–81. Supreme political control lay in Charles' own hands.

---

1   Hughes Oliphant Old, *The Reading and Preaching of the Scriptures in the Worship of the Christian Church: Volume 3 The Medieval Church* (Grand Rapids: Eerdmans, 1999), 188–92.

2   Edward James, 'The Northern World in the Dark Ages, 400–900,' in *The Oxford History of Medieval Europe* (George Holmes; Oxford: Oxford University Press, 1993), 95.

After 774 he never asked permission of the Pope to enter Rome, as kings had done previously.[3]

Second, against the Arabs, Charles, after a setback in 778 due to disunity among his Spanish supporters, successfully advanced into Spain in 793, establishing under his full control the Spanish March, a wide strip of land parallel with the Pyrenees. Further conquests followed in the next two decades, consolidating his power.[4] The Islamists were pushed back further from the main body of Europe.

Third, Bavaria—virtually independent on Charles' accession—was subdued in 781. Following an uprising six years later, Charles' troops invaded, Duke Tassilo surrendered and was reduced to a vassal. Further conquests followed to the east.[5]

Fourth, following a long history of conflict with the Saxons under Charles Martel and his successors, the Franks had become ascendant. At first Christian preachers met with little success and many were martyred. The Saxons were divided into many small political units. As Seeliger comments, they owed a fatalistic and fanatical obedience to the will of their gods.[6] After a military victory in 772, Charles quelled a revolt in 776 and compelled the Saxons to accept the Christian faith. The hostages he took in battle were trained in Christian teaching in order to be missionaries to their own people. In 780 he formally joined the Saxon lands to the empire. Two years later, in 782, he had passed a series of ordinances (the offenses proscribed tell a story of the prevailing circumstances in Saxon lands): death to any who broke into, robbed or set fire to a church, to any who ate meat in Lent, for the murder of a bishop, priest, or deacon, for

3 Gerhard Seeliger, 'Conquests and Imperial Coronation of Charles the Great,' in *The Cambridge Medieval History* (Cambridge: Cambridge University Press, 1936), 2:598–603.

4 Seeliger, 'Conquests,' 2:604–6.

5 Seeliger, 'Conquests,' 2:606–9.

6 Seeliger, 'Conquests,' 2:610.

burning another human being, cannibalism, cremation, human sacrifice, and for omitting to be baptized. The death penalty for these offenses could be set aside if the offender fled to a priest, offered confession and was ready to do penance. These draconian measures probably encouraged the rebellion that followed from 783–5. In suppressing the revolt, Charles—on one day—had 4,500 Saxons beheaded. The leaders of the uprising were baptized. The Pope ordered celebrations and thanksgivings all over Christendom at the successful end to a war of thirteen years. Church organization followed all over Saxon territory.[7]

Later, in 808–11 Charles conquered the Danes and the Serbs. By the end of his reign—he died in 814—the empire extended to the North Sea and Denmark, and to most of Italy in the south. His influence extended as far as Britain, where he was acknowledged as a Christian ruler. The Caliph put the place of the holy sepulchre at Jerusalem under his authority.[8]

Character

Charles' skeleton was 6' 4" tall—almost gigantic for the times. According to his ninth century biographer Einhard he had a round head, a thick but short neck, and a kindly face with quick eyes. He was corpulent and liked to eat large quantities of food. He drank moderately from large wooden cups filled with wine. He enjoyed music and usually had a book read aloud while he was eating. He enjoyed riding, hunting, and swimming.[9] In summer, he generally took a rest at midday. He often stayed awake at night because his mind was at work. He was kind and amiable with a keen sense of humour. He had a charismatic personality. He loved children. He kept his family life private. On the other hand, he was passionate and a womanizer—and accustomed

---

7   Seeliger, 'Conquests,' 2:610–13.
8   Seeliger, 'Conquests,' 2:615.
9   James, 'Northern World,' 94.

to command. Seeliger remarks that his immorality was notable even in an age as coarse as his.[10]

However, despite his passionate nature he never made decisions in angry moments. Thus his actions were strong and secure. He had a wide range of interests and an understanding of people's needs unique among the greatest leaders of history. He had a mastery of German and Latin, knew Greek, but was not himself a scholar, linguist or abstract thinker.[11] He could not understand the complexities of church dogma. But the teaching of the church was, for him, unassailable truth. He thus placed himself at the service of the Christian faith and also saw in Roman civilization a unifying source in his quest for power.

Charles' overriding concern was to rule an empire that was united and cohesive. A restoration of Roman culture was a key element in this but, even more so, was a common allegiance to the Christian faith. His plans were for the conversion and Christianization of the empire. For this he saw it was necessary for consistent Christian preaching and teaching in every parish church in Europe on every Sunday. But in a world as barbaric and illiterate as his, where the vast bulk of the clergy were incapable of carrying out this task, this was an enormous undertaking. To get anywhere near this goal, there needed to be a vanguard of Christian scholars, a widespread and effective educational drive, and authoritative implemented regulations requiring regular preaching and church attendance.

CHURCH AND STATE

There was an inseparable connection in Charles' mind between his rights and duties as a ruler and the functions of the church. This was seen in three episodes in the middle of his reign. First,

10 Seeliger, 'Conquests,' 2:626–28.
11 James, 'Northern World,' 94.

after the Saxon surrender in 785 he issued a capitulary, a decree, for the conquered territory, with the following provisions: execution for whoever enters a church by force, kills a bishop, priest or deacon, or cremates a body (ordinary homicide was at the time punishable by a fine). A minor capitulary required all people to pay a tithe to the church, and made it mandatory for children to be baptized within the year.[12] Second, a further capitulary was issued in 794 in which the church received most attention. Current heresies, such as adoptionism, were condemned, the powers of metropolitan bishops were confirmed and clarified, clerics were forbidden to move from one church to another without special permission, bishops were to avoid involvement in worldly affairs, monks were to live by the Rule of St Benedict, and clergy were to be tried for secular offenses in a court over which a bishop was to preside.[13] Third, there was the famous incident when Charles visited Rome in 800 and entered St Peter's on Christmas Day. Probably against his own wishes, the Pope thereupon crowned him Holy Roman Emperor.

This conviction is also evident in the relations that existed with the papacy throughout his reign. When Pope Leo III acceded in 795, Charles wrote to him (most likely a letter composed by Alcuin in Charles' name): 'It is my duty by divine aid to defend everywhere the holy church of Christ externally with arms against inroads by pagans and ravaging by unbelievers...it is your task, holy father, to support our fighting by hands raised to God as those of Moses.'[14] From around this time there exists a mosaic in the refectory of the Lateran in which St Peter sits on the throne with the keys of the kingdom of God, while on his right and left kneel Pope Leo and Charles respectively. To Leo

---

12   Donald Bullough, *The Age of Charlemagne* (second ed.; London: Elek, 1973), 94–95.

13   Bullough, *Charlemagne*, 96.

14   Bullough, *Charlemagne*, 94.

St Peter hands the pallium, to Charles the banner of the city of Rome. An inscription states, 'Holy Peter, you bestow life on Pope Leo, and victory on King Charles.'[15] This arrangement was greatly to Charles' advantage.

In one capitulary Charles likens himself to King Josiah, endeavoring to bring back to the service of God the kingdom entrusted to him by God.[16] In comparing himself to Josiah, Charles saw his task as a reformer rather than an innovator.[17] Even in matters of doctrine Charles often took the initiative, rather than the Pope. In 809 he ordered the retention of the *filioque* in the Western liturgy, against papal actions. The Franks had retained the clause but Rome had abandoned it in deference to the Greeks. Here Charles forced the Frankish rite to supersede the Roman. This action was theologically of a piece with his vigorous opposition to the Spanish adoptionism that was a matter of grave controversy at the time. It was against such adoptionism that the *filioque* had first been approved formally by the Synod of Toledo in 589.

In 795, shortly after his accession, Leo III did homage to Charles as overlord, pledging fidelity to him. Charles in turn gave the Pope a strict warning to lead an honourable life and to observe the teaching and decrees of the church. In 800, Alcuin wrote that the three highest powers in the world were the papacy, the empire as the second Rome, and the royal dignity of Charles. Charles precedes them all since he surpasses them in power, wisdom, and dignity, as he is appointed by Jesus Christ as the leader of the Christian people, the ruler of the kingdom of eternal peace founded by the blood of Christ. For Charles, the Augustinian dualism of two cities is no more. Charles' rule is not

15   Seeliger, 'Conquests,' 616.

16   Friederich Kempf, *The Church in the Age of Feudalism* (London: Burns and Oates, 1969), 71.

17   Rosamond McKitterick, *The Frankish Church and the Carolingian Reforms, 789–895* (London: Royal Historical Society, 1977), 2–3.

over a purely earthly kingdom, for it is identical with the earthly portion of the church, founded by Christ.[18] In short, Charles saw himself as called by God to found the kingdom of God on earth.

We need only recall that after the second Council of Nicaea in 787 had ended the iconoclast controversy by reinstating the use of images, Charles required the then Pope to excommunicate the Greek emperor as a heretic, even though the Pope was on the side of the Greeks! The Pope went ahead and did so—not daring to oppose Charles, he was forced instead to repudiate the second Council of Nicaea!

To advance his plans for the reform of church and society, Charles recruited the best scholars he could find. The chief of these was Alcuin (c. 735–804), who entered Charles' court in 781. He came from York and was an Anglo-Saxon, educated in the famous cathedral school at York, becoming its master in 766. In the line of Northumbrian Christianity from Bede, where a high level of Christian scholarship was cultivated, Alcuin was the prime force in the outburst of scholarly reforming activity that launched the Carolingian age.

CAPITULARIES

In 789 Charles issued the *Admonitio generalis*. This document contained complete proposals for the reform of the church. Charles was reluctant to trespass on the domain of the clergy and did so by characterizing himself as king Josiah, in the way that king promulgated the Deuteronomic laws to Judah. He saw himself as akin to an OT king restoring the true religion, turning his people away from idolatry.[19] He viewed himself as a royal contributor to the revival of religion and society. His decrees

---

18   Seeliger, 'Conquests,' 628.
19   Kempf, *Church*, 71.

were intended to preserve the special character of the church, not to intrude upon it.

The first 59 chapters of the *Admonitio generalis* contain decrees of the early church councils as transmitted by the collection recently brought from Rome.[20] The second section is particularly important, laying the foundation for the instruction and training of both clergy and laity. It consists, as Bullough remarks, of a series of practical exhortations drawn from the Bible. The first and most urgent requirement was that the Christian faith be preached by bishops and priests to the people. Then followed an outline of social virtues. There was to be peace, unity and concord among Christians. Those in authority should judge justly and not accept bribes. Various moral transgressions were condemned. The people were to be taught the value of faith, love of God, humility, patience, chastity and continence. The only right way for the Franks was to be the Christian faith. The ten commandments are prominent, not surprising since the kingly role of Josiah undergirds it all.[21]

The remaining sections deal with the role of the priesthood. The clergy should be diligent in their pastoral work, rooting out pagan practices and observing the church canons. Charles goes further and insists that the bishops and priests teach the people, confirm them as Christians and outlaw heathen customs. The teaching role was to dominate in all later decisions. Paganism was to be replaced. The people were to be baptized, taught the Lord's prayer, taught to sing the psalms properly, taught to understand the Christian faith and given communion. Since Christianity was complex, it was essential that the people be taught it thoroughly. This section is full of moral regulations directed at clergy of all ranks. Let there be schools in which the boys can read. Detailed

20   For a detailed discussion of the whole of the *Admonitio,* including what follows, see McKitterick, *Frankish Church,* 5ff; Bullough, *Charlemagne,* 115–16.

21   Kempf, *Church,* 72.

attention is to be paid to the psalms, musical notation, office and mass chants, chronological works, works on grammar and the catholic books.

The people were to be taught to look after the church buildings, to keep them clean and in good repair, to attend services regularly and not to leave before the benediction. Priests were told their pastoral and teaching tasks were equally important. They were to live godly, righteous and sober lives, encouraging others to the service of Christ by their example. As James points out, this was the first time in the west that 'Church and State united to bring Christianity to all under their control.'[22] It was a comprehensive plan for the rebuilding of the church and society.[23]

The conditions of the time must be recalled, since the prevailing background to these enactments was decadence. As McKitterick comments, society was half-barbarous, with only a veneer of Christianity and basically still pagan. Scholarship existed in isolated pockets. Thus the people were to stop work on Sunday, to gather in church to praise God, to receive the sacraments, while the priests were to teach the people, instructing them in the articles of faith and in Christian living. The worldview taught focused on Christ and redemption, rooted in the Bible and the creed of the church.[24] The *Admonitio* stressed that the salvation of the people rested in this. According to Bullough, if it is to be measured by the number of schools created, Charles' plans were ultimately a failure. But on the basis of other evidence, the Carolingian renaissance largely determined the intellectual and literary development of medieval Europe.[25]

Many of Charles' further actions were grounded on the requirements of the *Admonitio generalis*. Church councils too

22   James, 'Northern World,' 97.
23   McKitterick, *Frankish Church*, 4–5.
24   McKitterick, *Frankish Church*, 8–9.
25   Bullough, *Charlemagne*, 116.

followed in tune. The Council of Frankfurt (794) held it was false to believe that God can be prayed to only in Latin, Greek and Hebrew. The regional Council of Tours (813) asked for homilies to be translated into the Latin of the common people (the *rustica romana lingua*) so they could be understood by all.[26] There is evidence that the Lord's prayer and the creed were translated into the local vernacular in Allemania before 800, the Lord's prayer into Bavarian in the early ninth century, while the creeds and the Lord's prayer were available in the Rhine-Frankish dialect at around 800.[27] Shortly after Charles' death, many such manuscripts existed, including other vernacular texts for laity, which included baptismal vows. The Old Saxon *Heliand*, composed soon after 814, is widely regarded as the most outstanding piece of Carolingian religious literature. It tells the gospel story as a serial epic, with Christ as a war leader, his followers as warriors under his direction. According to Bullough, during Charles' reign there developed greatly improved standards of access to and use of Latin, a wider range of words available to the literature, a significant growth in literacy, and an improvement in both the appearance and practicality of scripts and manuscripts.[28]

Later in 802, in a special capitulary, Charles made obedience to the Christian God and the leading of a Christian life a test of loyalty to him. McKitterick points out that this was an extension of the feudal oath. Since Charles saw himself as God's agent, loyalty to both was intertwined.[29] Towards the end of his reign, an important development was that church legislation was more often introduced by the clergy rather than the king. The reform councils of 813 cite Charles as the author of a number of their

26   Bullough, *Charlemagne*, 116–17.
27   Bullough, *Charlemagne*, 116–17.
28   Bullough, *Charlemagne*, 118.
29   McKitterick, *Frankish Church*, 10.

canons but in fact Charles did not attend these councils in person but simply confirmed a report of the proceedings that was sent to him. He allowed the bishops to assume greater initiative and responsibility as time passed. Some scholars consider this to be Charles' greatest achievement.[30]

How far were these fine-sounding words implemented? Manuscript evidence from later in the ninth century suggests that many of these admonitions had penetrated deep into Frankish society. The records of cathedral and monastery libraries in the late ninth century indicate that the capitularies were preserved widely in writing, often in ordinary bindings, indicating their use on an everyday basis as a pedagogical rather than a legal tool. This suggests strongly that they were considered as manuals for the conduct of the clergy and thus of practical, everyday usefulness. Moreover, the greater proportion of books published during this time are texts of the Bible, gospel books, psalters, works of the Fathers, and such like, while the libraries were designed specifically to meet the needs of the schools. This is in line with the aims and intentions of Charles' capitularies. McKitterick comments that there is indicated 'a real connection between the wishes expressed by the monarch in the general admonitions for the provision of books and the books actually produced'.[31] It seems that every bishop and priest was able to have a copy of the canons to which he could refer.[32] The miscellaneous collections of capitularies were frequently bound in a plain fashion 'designed for practical, workaday use'.[33] She concludes 'Not only were the cathedral and monastic libraries gradually stocked with the theological and liturgical books necessary for intellectual and spiritual growth. There was also a definite, if diffuse, attempt to

---

30   McKitterick, *Frankish Church*, 12–14.
31   McKitterick, *Frankish Church*, 27.
32   McKitterick, *Frankish Church*, 32.
33   McKitterick, *Frankish Church*, 35.

possess the most important of the royal and ecclesiastical texts, that is, the texts which contained the programmatic schemes for the shaping of the *communitas fidelium* and the necessary directives, instructions, and definitions for the better implementation of administration, instruction and moral guidance'.[34]

PREACHING

Charles planned for expository preaching, teaching the content of the Christian faith in every parish church in the empire on every Sunday. He envisaged the whole of Europe united, speaking Latin and professing the Christian faith with understanding. At the heart of this was the liturgy and at the heart of that was preaching. This entailed missionary preaching. The Saxons in particular were converted from paganism to Christianity. Alcuin stressed the great commission in Matthew 28:18–20 (the passage was not called 'the great commission' until late in the nineteenth century) with its requirement of teaching as an integral part of missionary work. Due to the enforced nature of the Saxons' conversion, Charles was aware there were masses of uninstructed semi-pagans in the church. Introductory preaching and teaching were still needed. Hitherto preaching had only occurred on feast days, not only in the Frankish territory but generally in the Western church since at least the time of Pope Gregory the Great (c. 600). Moreover, when it happened, more likely than not it took the form merely of the reading of a written homily. In 785 Charles decreed that everyone in the empire was to attend church every Sunday and on all holy days and hear the preaching of the word of God. The bishops were instructed to ensure that in every parish church the priest was to preach on *every* Sunday and holy day. He was also concerned with the content of what was preached. The bishops must ensure that the priests preached

---

34   McKitterick, *Frankish Church*, 44.

Scripture, not their own ideas,—basic Christian doctrine, the creed, the Lord's prayer and Christian virtues. It was, as Old comments, to bring catechetical preaching into the heart of the church's life.[35] This was obviously a herculean task, one that could hardly be accomplished in a short time, given the parlous state of education and literacy of the day.

In order to establish this, Charles had to make extensive provision for the education of the clergy, without which a regular preaching ministry, Sunday by Sunday rather than merely on feast days, could scarcely be sustained. To this end, Alcuin revised the old Roman lectionary, producing a critical and updated version. This was particularly important after the barbarian invasions had wiped out the educated classes and drastically reduced the standards of the clergy. What preaching there was would consist of reading a sermon from the homiliary, a book of sermons of the Fathers together with aids for producing a simple homily. Charles wanted a lectionary, detailing a comprehensive system of readings of Scripture for church services, to cover every Sunday of the Christian year, as well as the holy days. Old remarks that without a lectionary there could not be a homiliary and without a homiliary there could not be preaching.[36] Alcuin's revised lectionary has been the basis for worship in the Western church ever since.[37]

Next in order was the expansion and development of the homiliary, drawn up by Paul the Deacon (c. 720–c. 800). Paul, whose real name was Paul Warnefrid, came from a prominent Lombard family. The sermons he included were more sermons for parish churches than monasteries. Paul gleaned material from the Fathers, using it as a basis from which to build sermons applicable throughout the Christian year. His homiliary contains 244 sermons, multiple copies for each occasion—including

---

35   Old, *Reading and Preaching: Volume 3*, 190.
36   Old, *Reading and Preaching: Volume 3*, 192.
37   Old, *Reading and Preaching: Volume 3*, 194–97.

samples from Augustine, Leo the Great, Gregory the Great, Bede, and Chrysostom. Paul helped shape the preaching of the Western church for centuries. He was a major architect of the sermon. Most preachers were at best barely literate, with little oratorical skill. This enabled them to preach the word of God to their congregations. It also encouraged others later to publish their sermons and so led to a long-term development of preaching.[38]

Following all this, Haimo of St Auxerre (c. 790–c. 855) wrote several commentaries (on the Pauline epistles, Revelation, the Song of Solomon, and the minor prophets), and a huge work *Homiliae de tempore*, a homiliary for the whole Christian year—a compendium of sermon aids to help other preachers preach. This was used for several centuries. It contained homilies for every single Sunday in the Christian year. The notable lack over previous years in sermons on the cross and resurrection of Christ was remedied by Haimo.[39]

According to McKitterick, writing on the preaching of the time following the *Admonitio generalis*, 'a feature of most of these sermons is the total lack of association with any larger community or society than that to which the sermon is first addressed.' They lack specific address to a lay dignitary and 'were also no vehicles for government 'propaganda', for there are few exhortations to obey an earthly ruler, loyalty being rendered rather to the 'king of heaven."' Indeed, there appears an indifference on the part of the church to public and governmental affairs. This undermines any notion that Charles intended comprehensive preaching throughout the empire as a means of political and social control.[40]

Homilies were set out precisely to follow Charles' decree that everyone be taught the Christian faith. Preaching, in fact, carried out the instructions of the *Admonitio generalis* to the letter,

38   Old, *Reading and Preaching: Volume 3*, 198–200.

39   Old, *Reading and Preaching: Volume 3*, 216–18.

40   Rosamond McKitterick, *The Frankish Church and the Carolingian Reforms, 789–895* (London: Royal Historical Society, 1977), 113.

but the initiative for presenting the sermon and for preaching passed to the church. Generally sermons were expository and exhortatory in nature, with no attempts to venture into rarefied theology or doctrine. Congregations are reminded of their obligations as Christians. There is an absence of polemic or controversy, invective and accusation, which were the prerogative of the aristocratic or educated members of society, civil and clerical.[41] The pastoral functions of the priest and the care of his flock are continuously in evidence. The parish church thus became the really influential pivot on which Frankish society revolved. In a time of political disintegration the church provided a sense of cohesion and ideological continuity, guidance in social behavior and ethics, and provision for humanity's spiritual needs.[42]

LONG TERM IMPACT

Seeliger remarks that for centuries Charles' policies gave direction to the historical development of the middle ages. This was the first great expansion of the idea of the State in the Christian West,[43] laying the basis for the later emergence of the nation state. While many today may balk at church reforms, no matter how right and beneficial they may be, being based on military conquest and royal decrees, there can be little doubt that in the context of the time and the prevailing feudal culture, this was a stellar way to prepare the ground for the widespread preaching and teaching of the gospel.

The emergence of Carolingian script in place of the Merovingian writing made manuscripts far more easy to read. It was a quantum technological breakthrough in the production of documents, next only to the invention of the printing press,

41   McKitterick, *Frankish Church*, 113.

42   McKitterick, *Frankish Church*, 114.

43   Gerhard Seeliger, 'Legislation and Administration of Charles the Great,' in *The Cambridge Medieval History* (Cambridge: Cambridge University Press, 1936), 2:658.

over six hundred years later. As a result there emerged 'a generation of scholars—poets, historians, textual critics, theologians,
philosophers.'[44] A huge proportion of ancient manuscripts that
antedated 800 had been lost or became corrupted. The Carolingian renaissance preserved those that remained. In addition, of
manuscripts from 800 or before that existed then, 95% are still
extant today. Charles' reforms helped preserve the teaching of
the Fathers for future generations of the church.

Inevitably, most of Charles' plans were in the end aspirational.
Bullough comments that he could not eliminate violence,
corruption or incompetence from Frankish life.[45]

Charles' vision of universal biblical preaching to an audience
required to hear it seems to me to be in pursuance of the
command of Christ in Matthew 28:18–20. By reviving the sermon
and aiming for an educated clergy, his policies influenced the
church in the long-term. Without it, there could have been no
Reformation. As Old concludes, 'it was not his army that made
him the founder of Europe; it was his faith. It was a faith that
opened the way to understanding and encouraged learning, for
at its center was the Word…The Jesus in whom Charlemagne
believed was the very Word of God.'[46]

BIBLIOGRAPHY

Bullough, Donald. *The Age of Charlemagne*. Second ed.
    London: Elek, 1973.

———. 'Europae Pater: Charlemagne and His Achievements
    in the Light of Recent Scholarship.' *English Historical
    Review* 85 (1970): 59–105.

James, Edward. 'The Northern World in the Dark Ages,
    400–900.' Pages 59–108 in *The Oxford History of Medieval*

44   James, 'Northern World,' 97.
45   Donald Bullough, 'Europae Pater: Charlemagne and His Achievements
in the Light of Recent Scholarship,' *English Historical Review* 85 (1970): 89–90.
46   Old, *Reading and Preaching: Volume 3*, 188.

Europe. George Holmes. Oxford: Oxford University Press, 1993.

Kempf, Friederich. *The Church in the Age of Feudalism.* London: Burns and Oates, 1969.

McKitterick, Rosamond. *The Frankish Church and the Carolingian Reforms, 789–895.* London: Royal Historical Society, 1977.

———. *Frankish Kings and Culture in the Early Middle Ages.* Aldershot: Variorum, 1995.

Old, Hughes Oliphant. *The Reading and Preaching of the Scriptures in the Worship of the Christian Church: Volume 3 The Medieval Church.* Grand Rapids: Eerdmans, 1999.

Seeliger, Gerhard. 'Conquests and Imperial Coronation of Charles the Great.' Pages 2:595–629 in *The Cambridge Medieval History.* Cambridge: Cambridge University Press, 1936.

———. 'Legislation and Administration of Charles the Great.' Pages 2:655–84 in *The Cambridge Medieval History.* Cambridge: Cambridge University Press, 1936.

5

ANSELM (1033–1109)

HISTORICAL CONTEXT

After the fall of the Roman Empire, Western Europe went into decline from around 500 until 1050, apart from a short spell under Charles the Great and in his immediate aftermath. A corollary of this was a reduction in population, which of itself had a depressive effect on economic, social and political life. Learning was almost eliminated, except for the monasteries, where the reforms under Charles were still preserved. Life was reduced to a battle against the elements and disease. However, from 1050 a change took place. The climate changed, a period of two and a half centuries of warmer temperatures allowed the growing season to extend. The population started to increase. Towns grew. Economic activity increased and the beginnings of a more sophisticated money economy emerged. This led to the development of nation states and of Europe itself, together with a growing optimistic outlook which affected the whole of European society. From 1050 until the dawn of the fourteenth century the church moved into a powerful and central place in the revitalized society. The rediscovery of a vast bulk of the writings of Aristotle encouraged a revival of learning. Eventually, in the thirteenth century there emerged cathedral schools and Universities, especially at Paris, Glasgow, and Oxford. Scholasticism or school learning developed, with reliance on Aristotle and placing a high valuation on human reason. Anselm lived at the start of this era and has been called 'the father of scholasticism.'

LIFE

Anselm lived from 1033–1109. He was born in Italy, at Aosta in Savoy, the son of a Lombard nobleman. He left home early in life and crossed the Alps, eventually reaching the Benedictine abbey of Bec, in Normandy. Its prior, Lanfranc, was internationally known. Bec was at this time one of the most prominent centres of learning in Europe. Anselm studied there and eventually taught. He liked Bec since it was quiet and gave opportunity to study in obscurity. At the age of 27 he became a monk.

Three years later, in 1063, Lanfranc moved to the monastery at Caen as prior and Anselm succeeded him as prior at Bec. Anselm immersed himself in the Fathers, Scripture, Augustine and the liturgy. He fasted unsparingly until he became emaciated. He stayed up late at night giving counsel. Some at Bec resented his rapid rise to prominence but he won them over by his peaceable conduct. His main problem was the administrative duties, which kept him from the serious business of life.

In 1066 William the Conqueror invaded England and appointed Frenchmen to leading positions. He made Lanfranc Archbishop of Canterbury. Until Lanfranc's death Anselm was the leading light at Bec. He became abbot in 1078 although he was reluctant to accept the task and implored his brothers to find someone else. Avoid office if you can, Anselm said. In his case he feared that the responsibilities would interfere with his scholarship. For him reading, reflection and prayer were inseparable. He delegated as much as possible and spent the time in scholarship and in watching over the spiritual and intellectual growth of the monks.

In 1089 Lanfranc died. Anselm visited England, urged by several in the nobility there, who were of course Norman French. The Archbishopric had remained vacant for several years. William II—William Rufus—enjoyed the revenues himself. Eventually he fell ill and in fear of hell was persuaded to fill the position. He chose Anselm. Anselm resisted the appointment and had to be installed by force. At Gloucester in March 1093, where the king was staying at the time, his fingers were forcibly prized open and the episcopal staff rammed into his hand. He was carried into the cathedral while the *Te Deum* was being sung. He protested that his appointment was invalid, but to no avail. He was enthroned at Canterbury in late September and consecrated one month later by the Archbishop of York.

Anselm's time as Archbishop, which lasted until his death, was marked by turmoil. In particular, he was in almost constant conflict with the two kings who reigned during this period. Anselm had a strong sense of church hierarchy and his responsibility to submit to the Pope as head of the church. The English church had always enjoyed a strong degree of autonomy, being governed by regular synods under royal protection. These conflicts were part of the Investiture Contest which had come to a head earlier on the continent in 1075–7 but had never been resolved. This was a church-state problem concerning the boundaries of jurisdiction.

In 1075 Pope Gregory VII (Hildebrand) claimed spiritual jurisdiction over the Holy Roman Emperor, Henry IV. The controversy flared up over the church of Milan, which regarded itself as virtually the equal of Rome. In a letter in December Gregory accused Henry of disobeying apostolic law concerning lay investiture in Milan and other important sees. He argued

that it was absurd to contend that the Pope did not have
jurisdiction over him. If that were so, Henry would not be a
Christian and could no longer be Emperor. Henry reacted by
calling a synod at Worms in January 1076 that deposed Gregory
as Pope, antagonizing large forces in Germany and Italy by
doing so. Gregory responded quickly and the Lenten Synod that
year in Rome excommunicated Henry and suspended him as
Emperor. Gregory wrote in his papal letter that the Act of the
Council excommunicating Henry also entailed his deposition
as Emperor. Thus, he released the people from their oath of
allegiance to Henry. He asked them to show mercy if Henry
repented. If he did not, another was to be elected Emperor in
his place. Gregory asked to be informed of such an election, so
he could confirm it. For his part, Henry claimed that he and the
bishops who supported him had the right to sit in judgment on
the Pope. Gregory regarded the actions at Worms as sedition.

Eventually, in 1077, Henry met Gregory at Carnossa in Italy.
Standing barefoot as a penitent, Henry was absolved by the
Pope. He undertook to do justice according to the judgement
of the Pope and to make peace according to his counsel.
Nevertheless, the affair erupted again in 1080, when Gregory
again excommunicated Henry, but this time Henry succeeded in
having Gregory replaced as Pope.

Back in England, Anselm refused William funds to assist a
military campaign, while William refused permission for Anselm
to go to Rome to receive the pallium from the Pope, since
William did not recognize Urban II as Pope. Eventually Anselm
went without the king's permission. After he was gone for about
a year both the Pope and William died in 1099 (the latter in a
famous hunting accident in the New Forest, with Earl De La
Warr looking on!). The new king, Henry I, wrote to Anselm
begging him to return. Anselm, when he got back, informed
Henry about the correct procedure for investitures, which Henry
rejected out of hand. Eventually a compromise was reached but

Anselm's health was by now declining and he died a few years later. However, it is Anselm's thought that has had lasting impact and is still the subject of debate today.

THOUGHT

Basic principles

Anselm's theology can be summarized in two of his own phrases: *fides quaerens intellectum* (faith seeking understanding) and *credo ut intelligam* (I believe so that I may understand), the latter of which is borrowed from Augustine, who is his major source. In the preface to a small treatise called the Monologion he makes two important statements that crystallize his thought. First, he claims to set out what follows (on the trinity) not on the basis of Scripture but solely on the basis of reason—and this at the request of his fellow monks. Second, he says that nothing he writes in the treatise is at variance with Augustine. Essentially, he aims to give a rational explanation of the Christian faith, dependent on Scripture, church dogma and Augustine. His use of reason stems from his prior theological commitment. It is an explanation for what is already believed.

'The Proslogion'[1]

This book was written in 1077–8, long before Anselm crossed the channel to England. The purpose is to produce one argument, requiring no other argument to support it, to demonstrate the necessary existence of God. This was written for his fellow monks. It has often been called the ontological argument for the existence of God. In this way it is put into a similar category as other arguments intended to prove God's existence to a sceptical

---

1 Eugene R. Fairweather, *A Scholastic Miscellany: Anselm to Ockham* (New York: Macmillan, 1970), 69–93; Brian Davies, *Anselm of Canterbury: The Major Works* (Oxford: Oxford University Press, 1998), 82–104.

and unbelieving audience. However, it is quite inappropriate to describe it this way. In this work, Anselm assumes God's existence and is seeking one argument to demonstrate rationally his necessary existence. Moreover, the book is couched in a context of prayer and devotion. He is addressing his fellow monks. He does not argue for the existence of God in contrast to atheism but for the fact that God must exist and cannot possibly be conceived as not existing since he is the source of all other beings.

Anselm's purpose, as he states it in the prologue, is to find one argument, dependent on no other argument, to show that God truly exists and that he requires nothing else for existence, and yet all other things rely on him for their existence. The key to grasping how to approach his argument is that it was written under the persona of one trying to understand what he believes. Anselm was not attempting to persuade an unbeliever but to promote understanding among believers. Thus, the first chapter starts with prayer, citing Psalm 27—'I seek your face'—adding expressions like 'come now, O Lord my God'. He refers to Adam, sin, and exile. The language is from the Psalms. He asks God to reveal himself.

The argument

Crucial to the whole case is Anselm's statement, 'we believe that you are that than which nothing greater can be conceived.' This supposes that God is not merely the greatest being, besides whom there is none to compare. It extends to the point that God is the greatest being we can possibly conceive. It goes even further so as to affirm that it is impossible for us to conceive of a being greater than who God is. It is a statement to the effect that God is greater than our greatest thoughts, that he is greater than the most perfect being imaginable. He is greater because he exists and exists necessarily.

Anselm contends that even the fool understands that this concept exists in his understanding even if he does not understand the existence of God. It is clear that we are able to form this idea, so that the reality exists in our own mind of a being greater than anything that can be thought.

Moreover, since God is that than which a greater cannot be thought, he cannot exist in the understanding alone since if this were so he would not be that than which a greater cannot be thought, since if he did not exist in reality he would be less than one who did exist in reality. Therefore, since he is that than which none greater can be thought, he must exist in reality as well as in the human mind.

Therefore, God—that than which none greater can be thought—cannot be thought of as not existing. If he could be thought of as not existing he would not be that than which no greater can be thought. This follows from the point that a being that exists is greater than a being that exists in the human mind only. Existence is a necessary property of that being than which none greater can be thought. Since God is that than which none greater can be thought he must exist, since existence is a necessary property. Moreover, necessary existence is entailed in his being that than which none greater can be thought, since if it were possible to conceive of God's non-existence, he could not be that than which none greater can be thought. Only God can be thought of as necessarily existing.

Comment

Anselm's argument places God in a category of his own. All other existents have at some point not existed and they will not exist in the future. When existing, their existence is contingent, with the constant possibility of non-existence. Moreover, it is possible to conceive of their non-existence. In the case of God, he exists necessarily and so his non-existence is both impossible, and also impossible for us to conceive. This is so since, if that possibility did exist, he would not be that than which none greater can be thought and, if we conceive of the possibility of his non-existence, it is not God about whom we are thinking.

This is a radically different argument from later versions of the ontological argument. Moreover, its intention is different. As we noted—and it may be necessary to repeat this—it is not constructed with a view to persuading unbelievers of the existence of God. It is produced for the benefit of Amselm's fellow monks, who already believe, and is intended to supply a rational argument for God's necessary existence. Furthermore, it comes in the context of prayer. Anselm immediately states, addressing God in prayer, 'and you are that being.'

Guanilo's criticisms

A fellow monk, Guanilo, countered Anselm. He pointed out that a person may have an idea of a perfect island. That is an idea in the mind but it does not necessarily exist in reality. So merely to have the idea of a perfect being does not entail that such a being exists. Guanilo's counter-argument was effectively repeated centuries later by Immanuel Kant. Kant criticized Anselm on the grounds that one can think one has 100 dollars in one's pocket—around 100,000 dollars in today's currency—but the thought does not entail the reality. In both cases, Guanilo and Kant argue that there is a chasm between ideas and existence, between the thought and the reality.

However, two vital points must be remembered. First, for Anselm God's existence differs in principle from the existence of all other things. God exists necessarily but 100 dollars in the pocket—still less, an imaginary perfect island—does not. Ideas we may have of this or that in the created realm bear no relation to existence unless there is evidence to sustain them. In the case of God, understood as that than which none greater can be thought, necessary existence is intrinsic.

The strength of Anselm's argument is that he considers God to be in a class of his own. All other existents are dependent on his existence and, in turn, on his necessary existence. He is of an entirely different order than his creation. At a stroke, atheism is ruled out, since the god who atheists deny is not the God about whom Anselm—or the Bible—speaks. Insofar as he depends on revelation, Anselm is thinking in accordance with a strictly theological method, on the basis of the transcendent nature of God, and not in conformity with methods designed to explore elements of the creation.

Cur Deus homo? (Why God became man?)[2]

This treatise was written while Anselm was Archbishop, but it was finished in his exile in Italy and published in 1098. In it Anselm tries to prove on rational grounds (with the initial assumption 'as if Christ did not exist') the necessity for the incarnation and the atonement. He is careful to stress that God is under no necessity in this. There is no external force that requires God to act in a particular way. The kind of necessity he has in mind is twofold. In one sense, from our perspective, it is something necessary to human reason. On the other, it rests on the reliability of God, that if he wills something he does not retract it and what he wills is in accord with his own nature. In this case, the necessity arises from the character of God. Because of who he is, this is the way he acts.

For centuries one of the most common views of the purpose of the atonement had been that it was a transaction by God with the devil, by which the devil was duped into having Christ killed only to be thwarted by his resurrection. As a result, the human race, over which the devil had exercised dominion, was freed from his control. We know this as the ransom theory of the atonement. This book, Anselm's major achievement, represents a

2   Fairweather, *A Scholastic Miscellany*, 100–183; Davies, *Anselm*, 260–356.

colossal advance. Due to pressures of time, this does not represent the whole of Anselm's doctrine of the atonement but rather the part which he thought was most pertinent for those in his own day. It takes the form of a dialogue with a fellow monk called Boso. Boso states that while we should believe the deep things of the faith before we discuss them rationally, it is careless, once we are established in the faith, not to aim at understanding what we believe (CDH, 1:1).

The question Anselm addresses is why did God become man and restore life to the world by his death when he could have done this by another person or by an act of his will? What were the reasons impelling him to bring about our salvation by the incarnation and death of his Son? Anselm begins by asserting that it was fitting, or appropriate, that God should act in this way (CDH, 1:3). Fittingness is a common thread in much of Anselm's theology. It refers to what is right and suitable for God to do in terms of his own character. It also points to the idea of beauty, that God's works are in harmony with who he is and are also the best and most desirable.

A strong theme of necessity is present too. In large measure this is due to human sin. Only God could redeem the human race since, if it were undertaken by any other person, humans would owe him a debt and so would be a servant to that one (CDH, 1:5). Anselm is strong in arguing that, contrary to the ransom theory, the devil has no legal claim over the human race (CDH, 1:7). It is to God that we are under obligation. Through sin, humanity has withheld from God the honour that is due him. To dishonour God is sin. 'thus to sin is the same thing as not to render his due to God.' Our wills need to be subject to God's will—so not rendering honour to God dishonours him and this is sin. Since we have violated the honour due to God we must repay this honour (CDH, 1:11).

In order to be saved, our sins must be forgiven. This cannot be done by a mere pardon, for God's honour requires either that sin be punished or else satisfaction be made for it, a full reparation for the sin plus more to make amends for the assault on God's honour. Anything else would be out of accord with the order God has instituted: 'it does not belong to his freedom or kindness or will to forgive unpunished the sinner who does not repay to God what he took away' (CDH, 1:12). Therefore either man must render honour to God or punishment will follow (CDH, 1:13, 15). God cannot remit sin unpunished (CDH, 1:19).

In considering the satisfaction that humanity must make, Anselm argues that man must restore more than he has withheld plus he must conquer the devil, since in sin he has submitted unlawfully to the devil (CDH, 1:21). This is beyond human power, due to the greatness of the satisfaction required, together with human inability resulting from original sin (CDH, 1:22–3). That man is unable to effect such satisfaction is no excuse. The debt owed to God remains. Moreover, the inability to pay the debt is itself culpable, since it was incurred freely by human choice (CDH, 1:24).

Consequently, only God can achieve this but not under necessity or compulsion, for nothing can coerce him. It is an act of grace, freely chosen; the necessity is a necessity of preserving his honour (CDH, 2:4–5). However, at the same time a man must render it, one of the same race as we are. 'None except God can render it and no one but man owes it—it is necessary that the God-man render it' (CDH, 2:6). This God-man is under no obligation himself—it is an act of obedient, free, gracious fulfilling of the will of God, freely surrendering his life to death (CDH, 2:7).

Therefore he must be born, and born of a virgin who is purified from sin (CDH, 2:8). In short, he must be human, taken from Adam and born of a virgin. Anselm provides a curious reason.

> God can make a man in four ways: from man and woman, as constant experience shows; neither from man nor from woman, as he created Adam; from a man without a woman, as he made Eve; or from a woman without a man, which he has yet to do. Therefore,

in order to prove that this way is also within his power, and was deferred for this very purpose, nothing is more fitting than for him to take that man whom we are seeking from a woman without a man. Moreover, we need not discuss whether this is more worthily done from a virgin or from one who is not a virgin, but we must affirm without the slightest doubt that the God-Man ought to be born of a virgin.

To which Boso replies, 'You say what my own heart believes' (CDH, 2:8). Well said, Boso!

The incarnation and sufferings of Christ are therefore necessary as a satisfaction rendered to God's honour (CDH, 2:11–15). Christ died freely (CDH, 2:16–18). He 'freely offered to the Father what he would never have lost by any necessity, and paid for sinners what he did not owe for himself' (CDH, 2:18).

In summary, Anselm states

> God did not need to descend from heaven to conquer the devil, or to act against him by justice to deliver man. But God did require from man that he should conquer the devil, and that he who had offended God by sin should make satisfaction by justice. For God owed the devil nothing but punishment, and man owed him nothing but retaliation, reconquering him by whom he had been conquered; but whatever was required from man was due to God, not to the devil (CDH, 2:19).

EVALUATION

The central theme for Anselm is the satisfaction of divine honour. He also writes of the atonement as a conquest of the devil and as a moral example. There are hints of substitution but nothing explicit concerning expiation or the propitiation of God's wrath.

However, Anselm's main achievement, against the backcloth of the ransom theory, was to shift the focus from a supposed transaction between God and the devil to something occurring between man and God. In doing this Anselm not only developed doctrine, he founded an era. Moreover, be brought together the incarnation and atonement into one whole movement of God's grace in which the cross of Christ comes on to centre stage effectively for the first time.

Inevitably, there are unresolved questions. The argument seems to be based heavily on the feudal system where the notion of honour owed to a feudal lord is paramount. Still, God is in a certain sense the greatest lord and Anselm was applying the gospel to the culture and thought of his day—that may be why his argument seems a little arcane to us. That is the perennial problem that comes with any form of contextualization; to adopt the language and cultural expressions of a particular time is to distance oneself from all other times. However, the argument rests as much, if not more, on themes present in the developing penitential system. This had the merit (!) of focusing on sin and the need for repentance.

FOR FURTHER READING

Primary sources

Brian Davies and G.R. Evans, eds. *Anselm of Canterbury: The Major Works*. Oxford: Oxford University Press, 1998.

Eugene R. Fairweather. *A Scholastic Miscellany: Anselm to Ockham*. New York: Macmillan, 1970, 47–215.

Secondary sources

Karl Barth. *Anselm: Fides quaerens intellectum: Anselm's Proof of the Existence of God in the Context of his Theological Scheme*. London: SCM, 1960.

G.R. Evans. *Anselm*. London: Geoffrey Chapman, 1989.

Bradley G. Green, ed. *Shapers of Christian Orthodoxy: Engaging with early and Medieval theologians*. Nottingham: Apollos, 2010, 293–340.

David S. Hogg. *Anselm of Canterbury: The Beauty of Theology*. Aldershot: Ashgate, 2004.

6

THOMAS AQUINAS (1225–74)

HISTORICAL CONTEXT

From 500 to 1050 Western Europe was in decline. The population was reduced and, except for the monasteries, learning was almost eliminated. Life was reduced to little more than a battle against the elements and disease. Then from 1050 a change took place. The population began to increase, towns grew in size, economic activity developed, with the beginnings of a more sophisticated money economy. This led to the emergence of nation states and of Europe itself. From 1050–1300 the church moved into a powerful and central place in the revitalized society. Learning was revived, following the rediscovery and translation into Latin of the vast bulk of the writings of Aristotle. Cathedral schools and universities emerged in the thirteenth century, especially at Paris and Oxford. Scholasticism or school learning developed, with reliance on Aristotle, placing a high valuation on human reason. A confident, optimistic outlook spread through society.

It was a time of global warming before the little ice age of the fourteenth century heralded decline and disintegration.

LIFE

Into this increasingly dynamic society, Aquinas was born, although the exact date is uncertain, it probably being some time in 1225. He was born to a Lombard family in a castle near the town of Aquino, between Rome and Naples. At an early age he was sent to the abbey of Monte Cassino. From 1239 he studied at the newly founded University of Naples and there he enrolled in the Dominican order; his family reacted in horror, placing him under house arrest with an armed guard! The Dominicans and Franciscans were mendicants and attracted the urban poor. The Dominicans encouraged scholarship. I recall my church history professor, Dr. Clair Davis, summing up the difference between the two orders by Francis preaching to the birds and animals, whereas Dominic, when his studies were interrupted by a bird flying into his cell, captured it, killed it, cooked it, and ate it! Eventually Thomas escaped from house arrest and travelled to study under Albert the Great, a Dominican scholastic, at Paris and Cologne. He returned to Paris in 1252 and lectured at the University on the Scriptures from 1252–4 and on the *Sentences* of Peter Lombard from 1254–6. In 1256 he was appointed Professor of Theology, occupying one of two chairs allotted to the Dominicans. From 1259 to 1268 he was back in Italy, teaching at various locations, including Rome. In 1269 he returned to Paris, filling his former position until 1272, when he returned to Naples to organize the Dominicans for theological study. In 1274 Pope Gregory X summoned Thomas to attend the Council of Lyons and on the way there he died, at the Cistercian abbey at Fossanova on 7 March, aged 49.

Because the subprior at Fossanova was cured of blindness when he touched Thomas' body, the Cistercians were afraid that

Dominicans would come and steal the remains. The body was interred and disinterred several times during the next two years. The head was cut off and hidden, a hand was sent to his sister, while a finger embarked on a tortuous path across Europe. When Thomas was canonized in the next century the corpse had been reduced to a pile of bones from which the flesh had been removed by boiling. The saga continued but since 1974, thankfully, the various parts are together, buried at the Dominican church in Toulouse.[1]

Clearly, Thomas had a peripatetic career but his unremitting attention to study and writing allowed him to produce an amazing number of works in a short time. Absent-minded, modest and kind, Thomas was known as 'the dumb ox' since he spoke little. According to Davies, he did not share his mentor, Albert the Great's interest in the world around him; 'Albert could tramp around studying flies and ostriches, while Aquinas was hard to coax from his room.'[2] In addition to his studies, he preached extensively. In 1273 he had a mystical experience while saying Mass and suspended work on his *magnum opus*, the massive *Summa Theologia*, saying 'all I have written seems to me like so much straw compared with what I have seen and with what has been revealed to me.'

A list of his teachings was condemned shortly after his death, in 1277, at the instigation of a group of powerful Franciscans. Controversy surrounded him but he was canonized in 1323. Aquinas became the theological standard in 16th century, replacing Lombard. However, it was much later, as a result of the Papal encyclical *Aeterni Patris* of Leo XIII of 4 August 1879 that Thomism was given its highest accolade. The encyclical required

1   Ralph McInerny, *Thomas Aquinas: Selected Writings* (London: Penguin, 1998), ix.

2   Brian Davies, *The Thought of Thomas Aquinas* (Oxford: Clarendon Press, 1992), 15.

Christian philosophy as contained in the works of Aquinas to be taught in the schools in conformity with the teachings of the church. This ascendancy continued unchecked until Vatican II was opened in 1962.

MAJOR WORKS

First in line, we must mention Thomas' *Biblical Commentaries*. This may surprise many, but we recall that his first post was lecturing in Holy Scripture and we shall see that he maintained that Scripture is the highest authority in the church. Moreover, one of Aquinas' single most important and lasting contributions was his work on principles of biblical interpretation, summarized in the *Summa Theologia*.[3]

Summa Theologia
This vast work was a systematic summary of theology for novices. Written from 1264, it consists of the following: Part 1: God and creation, including human nature, and the intellectual life of man. Part 2, 1st part: man's final end, and moral themes. Part 2, 2nd part: virtues and vices. Part 3: Christ and the sacraments. The work is unfinished.

Summa contra Gentiles (4 books)
The Gentiles are those preoccupied with a naturalistic philosophy imbibed from Greco-Islamic sources. The University of Paris was a seed-bed of Averroeism (see later). Thomas attempts to show

3   For a discussion of Aquinas' work on the Bible and the impact of his study of Scripture on his theology, see Mark W. Elliott, 'Thomas Aquinas,' in Bradley G. Green, *Shapers of Christian Orthodoxy: Engaging with Early and Medieval Theologians* (Nottingham: Apollos, 2010), 346–54; Christopher T. Baglow, 'Sacred Scripture and Sacred Doctrine in Saint Thomas Aquinas,' in Thomas G. Weinandy, *Aquinas on Doctrine: A Critical Introduction* (London: T&T Clark, 2004), 1–25.

that Christianity rests on a rational foundation. The principles of philosophy do not necessarily conflict with Christianity. He gives much space to the existence of God—Aquinas is dealing with pagans, Jews and Muslims. He starts with truths that can be established by reason alone and proceeds afterwards to deal specifically with Christian doctrine.

In addition Aquinas wrote many *philosophical works*, including commentaries on Aristotle.

THOUGHT

The context
It was only in the years around 1250 that the real challenge of Aristotle was appreciated. Anselm, Abelard, and Lombard, living in the eleventh and twelfth centuries, had no access to Aristotle's major philosophical writings. When these were translated into Latin they seemed to pose a major threat to the unified view of reality Christianity sought. This challenge was particularly pointed as these works were translated from Arabic and mediated via Muslim interpreters.

Some major features of Aristotle that fed into the views of these interpreters were the following. First, knowledge is via the senses and thus is knowledge of particulars. This was a significant departure from Plato and so from the Platonic view of the world.[4] A second important element in Aristotle is causality. Relations between this and that are seen in predominantly logical categories. Thus relationships of cause and effect are pervasive. Taking these casual chains back by extensive regress, God becomes the first cause or, as Aristotle said, the unmoved mover. This was a challenge to Christianity and seemed on the

4 But see McInerny, *Selected Writings*, xxviii–xxxiv, who points out that the connection between Aquinas and Aristotle is not so straightforward as was often assumed and that Aquinas is also indebted in various ways to Plato.

surface more compatible with the Islamic view of Allah, with its fatalistic determinism.

Moreover, the church had for long associated Aristotle with Nestorianism. Nestorius, a fifth century heretic, stressed concrete historical reality, and thus the two particular natures of Christ, and again the visible appearance, the humanity of Christ. Nestorius wanted to do justice to the humanity of Christ but, in so stressing this, he jeopardized the unity of Christ's person. He posited two sons, the son of God and the son of Mary. In short, he was held to teach not an incarnational union but a conjunction, effectively between two persons. This was ruled to be heresy, since without a genuine incarnation we could not be saved. Exiled Nestorians, banished from the Empire, had preserved Greek culture, including Aristotle, in their schools in Syria, translating Aristotle into Syrian, Persian and Arabic from around 800. Once in Arabic, Aristotelianism spread through the Islamic world from Spain to India with the help of a number of leading interpreters: Avicenna (born in 980 in Persia) read Aristotle's Metaphysics forty times and didn't understand it until he memorized it verbatim!; Averroes (born in 1126 in Spain) had a deep influence on the West, more so than on Islam since Islamic theology was restricted to the Koran and opposed to philosophy; while Moses Maimonides (born in 1135 in Spain) was an Aristotelian scholastic and orthodox Jew! He wrote in Hebrew and Arabic arguing that the only way back to faith was by consistent use of scientific and philosophical arguments.

The West was overwhelmed by the power of this development. It could offer no real challenge. From 1210–63 came a long series of church admonitions, restrictions and bans against public lectures on Aristotle in the universities. This was not a straightforward polarization between church and academy, as many scholars were perturbed as well. Nor did the church want to be obscurantist. But its prohibitions were a dead letter. Aristotle was discussed freely and openly in the universities despite these edicts.

In Paris, Thomas was faced by a group of avant-garde pro-
fessors who from 1265 gathered round Siger of Brabant. Called
'Latin Averroists' or 'heterodox Aristotelians' they effectively undermined the traditional teaching of the church by propounding
a form of 'double-truth.'[5] It was claimed that something could
be true scientifically and philosophically while being false theologically. There is some doubt as to Siger's own position on this
but many held to this position. It opened the way to deny the
principle of conjoining, reconciling or integrating what was believed and what was known. A dynamic rationalism was gain-
ing ground and dominating the University of Paris. Reason was
assuming autonomy. No one was prepared to oppose it—until
Aquinas was recalled in 1268.

Faith and reason, philosophy and theology
According to Thomas, the object of faith is supernaturally revealed by God. Reason cannot by its own powers recognize God
as triune. Revelation is contained in the holy Scriptures. God is
the author of Scripture, revealing knowledge to the prophets,
confirming it by miracles and signs and by the spread of the true
faith. Our faith rests on the authority of Scripture. The authority
of those who teach and interpret it is subsidiary. This necessity
of revelation from Scripture is due to the weakness of our intellect rather than sin. On the other hand, the church needs to
interpret Scripture, since it contains revealed truth in an obscure
and diffused manner, which the church must state in a plain and
connected way. This has been done in the Apostles' creed, and by
the Councils of Nicaea, Constantinople among others and in the
writings of the Fathers.

Revelation is accepted by faith since reason is incapable of
comprehending it. Faith is essentially an act of the will, moved to
assent by the promise of a reward. The intellect responds to the

5   McInerny, *Selected Writings*, xxii.

impulse of the will. However, faith is seated in the intellect—as knowledge—and nothing can be willed before it is known. Faith is infused by God into the intellect (*habitus*) and as a result is active through the will (*actus*). The act of the will is crucial. Since it proceeds from the will, faith is meritorious, formed by love, since love is the acting of the will. Laymen have implicit faith— belief in what the church teaches—although explicit faith is required of all concerning the trinity, the incarnation and so on, for salvation is perfect knowledge. Faith, however, is incipient knowledge.

The revelation with which faith is concerned is above reason but is not contrary to reason. Therefore, it is not the task of theology to prove revelation by reason, for that is impossible. Theology shows that the Christian faith is not impossible; a useful point for refuting opponents like the Averroeists. But its knowledge is superior to and above that of all other sciences, for its object is God. It is speculative rather than practical.

Aquinas, in short, is concerned to express that what is believed is in full harmony with what is known so as to counter the Averroeists at the University of Paris. Moreover, stressing that it is a higher truth, not contrary to truth, he underlines that faith and reason are compatible. However, faith is basic. In this, he follows Anselm's principle, *fides quaerens intellectum*. In other words, Aquinas shows the limitations of reason. Aquinas' whole theology is an expression of this principle. He recognized an autonomy of reason in its own field but restricted its competence. In the context of his day he was moving in a positive direction.[6]

Universals

Aquinas' maxim, taken from Aristotle, was that nothing is in the intellect unless it is first perceived by the senses. We see objects

---

6   See Per Erik Persson, *Sacra Doctrina: Reason and Revelation in Aquinas* (Oxford: Blackwell, 1970).

through the senses. The intellect develops an idea of the universal, and the immaterial form is certainly what is ultimate. McInerny compares this with someone who has made a study of the earwig. In reply to a question of which earwigs, the author acknowledged that the ones he studied were now dead. Yet it was not so much dead earwigs or currently living earwigs, nor earwigs that would be born in the future but rather with 'the earwig' that he was concerned.[7] However, for Aquinas the particular comes first in order. He advocated, then, the *a posteriori* method of Aristotle rather than *a priori* method of Anselm. In this, the intellect is held in check and has a derivative role.

Thus a proof for the first cause is found by observing external reality and then *a posteriori* moving back to the existence of God. God is known not in himself but in his works.

As David Knowles wrote:

> The realms of reason and revelation became separate, and the bounds of theology and philosophy, faith and natural knowledge stood out sharp and clear. There is only one truth, but there are realms of truth to which the unaided human mind cannot attain...therefore it is not possible for a man to have faith and natural certainty about one and the same proposition, still less can faith and natural certainty be in opposition. Moreover, all being and therefore all truth comes from a single source; there is therefore an order and harmony in all the parts. In the celebrated and characteristic phrase of Aquinas: 'Grace does not destroy nature; it perfects her.'[8]

Analogical knowledge of God

Aquinas held that God alone is self-existent. His essence, or being, is beyond our knowledge. This raises the question of how can we say anything true of him, given that he is beyond knowledge? For

7   McInerny, *Selected Writings*, xxix.

8   David Knowles, *The Evolution of Medieval Thought* (New York: Vintage Books, 1964), 261–62; Thomas Aquinas, *Summa Theologica*, i, Q 8, a 1, ad 2.

instance, when we say that God is good, can we know how or in what way he is good? If our statements about God were equivocal, if the way God is good is so beyond us that it would be impossible for us to know, we would be reduced to agnosticism. In fact, the meaning of the word 'good' is the same whether we apply it to God or to ourselves. At the other extreme, our language about God cannot be univocal either; the way God is good and the way we are good cannot be precisely identical, since that would destroy the creator-creature distinction. Therefore, Aquinas concluded, our knowledge of God is analogical. In terms of statements about God being good, Aquinas argues that we know goodness from observing it in the creatures. On the other hand, God is infinitely good, without all the corrupting and distorting elements that enter into the concept on the creaturely level. The qualities of goodness are present in God incomprehensibly and inconceivably to us. Hence, we can talk about God, bearing in mind that there are aspects that are the same and aspects that are infinitely different.[9] This was a blow against the idea of double truth, for Aquinas was asserting that things in the world can have a certain correspondence with heavenly realities.[10]

God

We know the existence of God, his unity and attributes, by reason, by concluding from realities in creation that there is a creator. However, what kind of God this is, and the fact that he is trinitarian is something we know only by revelation through faith. Yet what is known of God through faith is 'fitting' with what is known of him in creation by reason. Again, there is no inherent contradiction between faith and reason, and so the idea of double truth is untenable.[11]

---

9   Aquinas, *ST*, 1, Q 13, a 5.
10   Mark W. Elliott, 'Thomas Aquinas,' in Green, *Shapers*, 360.
11   Green, *Shapers*, 364.

Christology

Aquinas had nothing remarkably new to say here, although some have questioned whether he did justice to the humanity of Christ. For example, he foreshadows Luther's later innovation, whereby the attributes of Christ's deity are held to have been communicated to the humanity.

Work of Christ

Aquinas wrote of Christ as the head of the human race or the church, focusing on the connection between Christ's atonement and its beneficiaries. He went beyond Anselm as he tried to combine Anselm's satisfaction theory with Abelard's supposed stress on moral influence.[12] Christ's satisfaction of divine justice was not merely sufficient, but superabundant.

Sin and grace

For Aquinas, man needs grace before the fall as well as after it. Adam had original righteousness and also a *donum superadditum* (a superadded gift of knowledge to instruct others) plus sanctifying grace seated in his soul. Original sin is the lack of this original righteousness. It is a state or condition. Depravity is not total, affecting every area of the human being. But self-redemption is excluded, for salvation must come from God alone. Grace is a supernaturally infused condition in the soul, in effect equated with the new nature given by the Holy Spirit. Man's free will cooperates as it is moved by God—a theme in

12   Peter Abelard (1079–1142) has usually been identified with the moral influence theory of the atonement. This is at least problematic. Its origin appears to lie more with the liberal theology of the late nineteenth century; see R.E. Weingart, *The Logic of Divine Love: A Critical Analysis of the Soteriology of Peter Abelard* (Oxford: Clarendon Press, 1970), 78–96, 125–26; R.O.P. Taylor, 'Was Abelard an Exemplarist?' *Theology* 31 (1935): 207–13; Alister McGrath, 'The Moral Theory of the Atonement:: An Historical and Theological Critique,' *SJT* 38 (1985): 205–20; Robert Letham, *The Work of Christ* (Leicester: Inter-Varsity Press, 1993), 166–67, 261.

Augustine—but Aquinas' stress is not on God working but on
the infused grace. In this, Aquinas gives greater scope for human
freedom and shows a subtle shift towards semi-Pelagianism.
He is 'a bit more optimistic than Augustine about the natural
capacity of humans for virtue.'[13]

Justification

Here in Aquinas' thought there are four elements. First, there
is an infusion of grace. Then, secondly, comes a movement
of the human free will towards God in faith. Thirdly, there is
also a movement of free will away from sin. Fourthly, is the
remission of guilt. The consequence of this paradigm is that
basically justification consists in the infusion of righteousness.
It is not forensic; not until 1530 did that clearly appear. For
Aquinas, justification relates to something wrought in us
rather than something done outside us by Christ. Since faith
is an act of the will, and assent to truth, justification by faith
is impossible since it would have left no room for good works.
The definition of faith needed to change before justification by
faith could be recognized. In this Aquinas was not alone. While
there are definitely prefigurements of the Protestant doctrine
of justification before the Reformation, the consensus—and
Augustine is at one with this—is that it relates to the whole of
the Christian life and so encompasses the change brought about
in us.[14]

Sacraments

Effectively Aquinas has the basis of the sacramental theology
of the Council of Trent. We note two important points: (1)
the materializing of grace—grace is contained in the material
elements, and (2) a hierarchical concept of the church—the

13   Green, *Shapers*, 357.
14   See Green, *Shapers*, 358–59.

sacraments are constituted by the priests who administer them. This stress on the sacraments means that Aquinas is rather less occupied with the cross.[15] However, he did come to appreciate that preaching was superior to the sacraments.[16]

The church

Aquinas called the church both the communion of the faithful (viewed as a hierarchy) and also one body (with one head—the pope). This remains a tension to this day. The idea of the church as the body of Christ has been used to buttress Papal authority, while the metaphor of the people of God has been used in support of the conciliar movement. Vatican II swung to the more democratic model but Pope John Paul II brought a more conservative reaction.

IMPACT

(1) *Apologetic.* In the context of the thirteenth century, Aquinas demonstrated that Christianity is compatible with reason and capable of rational explanation and defence. Moreover, he stressed that all truth is God's truth, whether apprehended by reason or faith. For Aquinas, the faith is not attained by reason but it can be rationally explained and defended. In short, he met the Aristotelian challenge. *He also demonstrated the limits of reason.* Some things can only be revealed and are intrinsically beyond the grasp of the unaided human intellect. This went counter to the rationalism of the Latin Averroeists.

(2) As Augustine and Calvin, Aquinas can be claimed by all sorts of people. With some of the caveats we have already noted, relating to church, sacraments and such like, overall his teaching

---

15 Green, *Shapers*, 377.
16 Green, *Shapers*, 347.

is sound, Christian and biblical, particularly when judged appropriately in historical context.

(3) *He helped rescue the church from the excesses of allegorical methods in the interpretation of Scripture.* For centuries biblical interpretation had been carried out under the shadow of Origen (185–254). Origen held that there were normally three layers of meaning in the biblical text. These corresponded to his tripartite view of the human constitution—body, soul, and spirit. The bodily sense of Scripture was the obvious, literal, historical meaning, suitable for the simplest sort of believer. The sense corresponding to the soul was the moral meaning, while the spiritual meaning was for the advanced Christian, effectively the spiritual elite. This referred to some relationship of the spirit and was not normally evident on a surface reading of the text.[17] This method lead to an excessive interest in allegory. Aquinas redirected biblical interpretation by arguing that the literal sense was what the author intended, whether this was literal, historical or spiritual. In turn, the literal meaning as he understood it might point to other realities beyond it. In doing this Aquinas brought biblical interpretation back to recognize that meaning in the text of Scripture is to be grounded on the intent of the author. In doing so he placed a brake on unchecked use of allegory.[18] It is difficult to calculate the benefit this brought over the coming centuries.

PROBLEMS

(1) *His dichotomy between reason and faith had unfortunate consequences.* One such problem was its effect on the Western church's view of the trinity. Reason leads us to theism but revelation alone makes known the trinity. In Aquinas himself

---

17   Origen, *On First Principles*, Book 4.
18   Aquinas, *ST*, 1, Q. 1, Art. 9–10.

this created a split between *de deo uno* (the one God) and *de deo trino* (the trinity), seen in both the *Summa Theologia* and the *Summa contra Gentiles*. This, it is claimed by some scholars, had baneful effects in the West.[19]

(2) *He played an important part in the development of the Roman dogma on the church, sacraments, and justification.* This helped to harden Rome against the Reform movement in the sixteenth century.

FOR FURTHER READING

Thomas Aquinas. *Summa Theologiae.* Blackfriars edition. New York: McGraw Hill, 1964. There is a concise, one volume, summary in English by Timothy McDermott, published by Westminster Press, 1989.

Brian Davies. *The Thought of Thomas Aquinas.* Oxford: Clarendon Press, 1992.

Mark W. Elliott, 'Thomas Aquinas,' in Bradley G. Green, ed. *Shapers of Christian Orthodoxy: Engaging with early and medieval theologians.* Nottingham: Apollos, 2010, 341–88.

Ralph McInerny, ed. *Thomas Aquinas: Selected Writings.* London: Penguin, 1998.

Thomas G. Weinandy, Daniel A.Keating, and John P. Yocum, eds. *Aquinas on Doctrine: ACritical Appreciation.* London: T&T Clark 2004.

---

19   See Colin Gunton, 'Augustine, the Trinity, and the Theological Crisis of the West,' *SJT* 43 (1990): 33–58. In contrast, note Stephen R. Holmes, *The Holy Trinity: Understanding God's Life* (Milton Keynes: Paternoster, 2012), 154–9.

7

MARTIN LUTHER (1483–1546)

BACKGROUND

Throughout the fifteenth century there was growing discontent with the Papacy and the failure of the church to reform itself. Abuses were rife. Absenteeism, where clerics held benefices but were never present to fulfill their duties, and pluralism, where a cleric held multiple posts with the associated income, were common. Papal interference in matters of both church and state was greatly resented. However, pressure for doctrinal reform was conspicuous by its absence.

The Papacy itself was weak. Due to unrest in Rome, it had decamped to Avignon from 1309–77, a period known as the Babylonian Captivity. When conditions improved sufficiently for a return to Rome, rival Popes were elected still at Avignon; this problem, known as the Great Schism lasted for over a generation, from 1377–1413. In the wake of this instability came the Conciliar movement of the early fifteenth century, when church councils took the initiative in directing the church. The Lateran Council (1512–17) failed to deal with the issues plaguing the church—it was effectively the last chance for Rome to set its house in order.

Simultaneously, nationalism was on the rise. The power of kings was increasing. Indeed, the Reformers were to look increasingly not to the church to reform itself but to the civil authorities to do it. Rapid economic changes led to the growth of cities, with the pressure for change that urbanization brings. Germany was economically prosperous, with a rising sense of nationalism, its geographical area almost identical with the Holy Roman Empire, but it was hopelessly divided into hundreds of tiny principalities.

It was an age of dissolving certainties. The powerful influence of nominalism, holding that reality is only to be found in particulars, brought the idea that we cannot know things in themselves but only in this or that particular instance. Hence, the question of how far we can know was a pressing one. At the same time, the Renaissance, with the growth of humanism and its basis in original sources and the invention of the printing press were to give impetus to the rapid dissemination of new ideas, a rediscovery of the past lending fuel to change in the present.

THE IMMEDIATE CONTEXT

Archbishop Albert of Mainz needed cash. He borrowed from the Fuggers in March 1515. As security he arranged that throughout the Empire the indulgence be proclaimed that the Pope had declared for the building of St Peter's in Rome. Money from the sale of this indulgence would go partly to the building of St Peter's, partly to the bankers. Buying an indulgence reduced one's ecclesiastical penalties in penance. The peasants thought they were reducing their time in purgatory; this was a more urgent matter for the populace than heaven or hell, since they believed that as baptized penitents heaven was their goal but that painful cleansing lay ahead beforehand.[1] Tetzel, a Dominican, proclaimed it. The Elector of Saxony, Frederick the Wise, banned him from his territory. He was jealous of Tetzel and wanted the money himself. But some crossed the border from Saxony to hear Tetzel preach and to buy his indulgences.

Luther

Born in 1483, the son of a mine owner in Saxony, Luther's father wanted him to study canon law. An experience in a severe thunderstorm led him to become a monk instead. In 1508 he was appointed Professor of Philosophy at the University of Wittenberg on the recommendation of Johannes Staupitz, his mentor who had directed him to depend on God's grace not his own works. In 1512 he became Professor of Biblical Studies. He lectured on Scripture and the Fathers.

His evangelical breakthrough

This is difficult to date. It happened some time between 1512 and 1517, probably in 1515–16 during his lectures on the Psalms, which show a significant change around Psalm 55 and 56. But it was not through the Psalms that this occurred. Luther's background is important here. He was educated in the *via moderna*, linked with the nominalism we described earlier. The most prominent figures were William of Ockham (1287–1347) and Gabriel Biel (c. 1425–95). In contrast to realism, nominalists denied the existence of universals. In terms of salvation, the *via moderna* held that God gives grace to those who *facere quod in se est* (do what is in them, or do their best).[2] The problem for Luther was how could he be sure that he had done what was in him?

---

1   See James Atkinson, *Martin Luther and the Birth of Protestantism* (1968; repr., Atlanta: John Knox Press, 1982), 141–49.

2   Heiko Augustinus Oberman, *The Harvest of Medieval Theology: Gabriel*

Towards the end of his life, Luther recalled that he understood the righteousness of God in retributive terms, as God punishing sinners and rewarding the righteous. He felt himself to be a sinner and 'raved on with a wild and confused conscience.' While reading Romans 1:17 he began to realize that what was in view there was God's soteric (saving) righteousness through which the merciful God makes us righteous through faith. 'Here I felt that I was altogether born again, and had entered paradise itself through open gates.'[3] So by October 1517 Luther was teaching justification by faith from the letters of Paul (although the imputation of Christ's righteousness did not feature until at least 1530 and was introduced not by Luther but by Melanchthon).[4] However, he was not alone, for Jacques Lefèvre d'Étaples' 1512 commentary on Romans had already taught it.[5]

The progress of his thought during the critical years 1517–21

(1) There is nothing in Luther's Ninety-five Theses, which he nailed to the door of the Castle Church at Wittenberg on 31 October 1517, that hints at what was to be Protestant teaching. His initial outburst was against Tetzel. He saw no reason to question the authority of the Pope, his naive optimism about Papal intentions betraying his ignorance of the wider world. In his Sermon on Indulgence and Grace preached on the same day he acknowledges the validity of the sacrament of penance. His point is that indulgences weaken penance.

Biel and Late Medieval Nominalism (Grand Rapids: Eerdmans, 1967); Heiko Augustinus Oberman, *Harvest*, 120–84.

3   Martin Luther, 'Preface to the Complete Edition of Luther's Latin Writings,' in *Luther's Works: Volume 34: Career of the Reformer, IV* (Lewis W. Spitz; 1545; repr., Philadelphia: Muhlenberg Press, 1959), 337.

4   Alister E. McGrath, *Iustitia Dei: A History of the Christian Doctrine of Justification: Volume II: From 1500 to the Present Day* (Cambridge: Cambridge University Press, 1986), 11–14.

5   Philip Edgcumbe Hughes, *Lefèvre: Pioneer of Ecclesiastical Renewal in France* (Grand Rapids: Eerdmans, 1984), 74–78.

(2) In October 1518—one year later—his interview with Cardinal Cajetan took Luther a stage further. The Dominicans (of which Tetzel was a member) had pressed for Luther's execution, since he was opposing papal authority. Luther denied he was opposing the Pope. In this interview Cajetan insisted that this was in fact the case. Luther resisted and did not recant his theses. He was smuggled out of Augsburg at night. As a direct consequence of this interview he was forced to abandon support for Papal authority. In November he appealed for a General Council. This was still an appeal on the basis of the authority of the church, in line with the conciliar movement of the previous century. So by early 1519 he recognized that supreme authority in the church rested with a General Council. However, this was no breach with Rome for many in the church shared this view. Its pedigree can be traced back at least to Cyprian (200–58).[6]

(3) The July 1519 Disputation with Eck proved decisive, held in Leipzig between Carlstadt and Eck. Eck was a brilliant controversialist and debater and had much the better of the battle. Luther joined in, in support of Carlstadt. Leipzig was close to Bohemia, the land of Jan Hus. Eck accused Luther of sharing Hus's views, which had been condemned as heresy, for which he was burned at the stake.Lacking debating skill, Luther conceded that Hus was right in some things and that the General Council of Constance was wrong in condemning him. This raised acutely the question of the locus of authority and drove Luther to look to Scripture as the supreme authority.

(4) Events in 1520–21 forced Luther into an open breach with Rome. Much German opinion consolidated behind him, fed by dislike at interference by Italian Popes in German affairs. On 15 June 1520 (almost a year after the Eck debate) the Pope issued a

6   See Cyprian, *On the Unity of the Catholic Church*, in The Rev. Alexander Roberts and James Donaldson, eds. *The Ante-Nicene Fathers: Volume 5* (rpr; Edinburgh: T&T Clark, 1990), 421–29.

bull *Exsurge Domine*, condemning as heretical 41 propositions of Luther, ordering his books to be burned, and giving him two months to recant or face excommunication. In December 1520 Luther burned the bull publicly at Wittenberg. In January 1521 he was formally excommunicated. The quarrel now affected not only the church but the Empire. In April 1521 the Diet of Worms was called by the Emperor Charles V. Here Luther refused to recant—'Here I stand, I can do no other' he declaimed. The ban of the Empire was placed on him—the Edict of Worms. All states were requested to destroy the heresy. Therefore Luther's progress to reform was a gradual one. The nailing of the ninety-five theses on the castle door at Wittenberg was one part of that movement but of itself it was a minor part.[7]

(5) The ending of the Roman mass at Wittenberg was not until 1526. This is generally regarded as the point in the Reformation at any one place when the breach with Rome is decisive ecclesiastically. This change had already occurred elsewhere, in places like Zürich and Strassburg.

Luther's literary output 1517–20

To the Christian nobility of the German nation (1520). This was both polemical and revolutionary. Luther called the princes and magistrates to reform the Church since it was incapable of doing the job itself. The basis for this is that all Christians are priests.

The Babylonish captivity of the church (1520). In this, Luther attacked the seven sacraments. Only three were biblical, he argued—baptism, penance and the Eucharist. In turn, he saw them no longer as a means of salvation but as means of grace.

Of the liberty of a Christian man (1520). Here his focus was justification by faith and its implications for the life of the

---

7   See Robert Letham, *Through Western Eyes: Eastern Orthodoxy; A Reformed Perspective* (Fearn: Mentor, 2007), 174–6.

Christian. This is conciliatory; it was Luther's last attempt to win the support of Rome.

Why was no action taken to stamp out Luther and his supporters?
Internally, Luther had the support of Elector Frederick the Wise, at first tacit then open. But could external forces have quelled his support? Here there were two main sources that could have curtailed the reform movement. First, there was the Pope, Leo X (1513–21) who happened to be complacent. For him, Luther was simply an obscure German monk objecting in academic fashion to indulgences. By the time he awoke to the threat it was too late. Most of Germany had rallied behind Luther and the matter had assumed nationalistic as well as religious dimensions. Second, was the Holy Roman Emperor. Charles V was not crowned until 1520, so from 1518–20 there was an interregnum, a power vacuum. Serious threats in the east from the Turks (who were close to Vienna) and from Francis I of France in the west—the Houses of Valois and Hapsburg were jealous and bitter rivals—distracted the Emperor. Moreover, the Empire was fragmented and disunited.

Events 1521–9
During this time there was a change from a protest movement to a system of churches.

(1) 1521–2 Wartburg. Elector Frederick had Luther kidnapped while returning from Worms and held for his protection. He spent the year in seclusion, suffering a minor nervous breakdown, seeing demons crawling around everywhere, throwing his ink-pot at the devil, and translating the New Testament into German.

(2) The Peasants War 1524–5. Throughout Germany there were riots and rebellions. In 1525 Luther wrote *Against the robbing and murdering hordes of peasants*. He urged princes to shed blood if needed. A rebel cannot be met with reason; the best way to deal with him is to punch him in the face until he has a bloody

nose.[8] His conservative social instincts are obvious. At this time widespread popular support for Luther collapsed.

(3) 1524–5 he had a breach with Erasmus over the bondage of the will. Luther had progressed beyond the moral reform for which the humanists yearned.

(4) Changes in the organization of the church took place. The sermon became the centre of worship rather than the Eucharist. Luther developed a distinction between the visible and invisible church. Excommunication was to be only for openly sinful acts. The magistrate preserved order in the church, enforcing doctrinal uniformity and supervising the morals of the clergy and the laity. In effect this was a state church supervised by the civil magistrate. Where tyranny occurred in society Luther argued it should be endured for charity's sake.

(5) New accessions to Lutheranism came from 1524–9. In 1525 Albrecht of Hohenzollern, in 1526 Philip of Hesse, in 1528 Brandenburg, Schleswig, Brunswick, and Mansfeld joined Luther's movement, while Nuremburg acceded before 1524, Strassburg, Ulm, and Augsburg from 1524–6, and Magdeburg in 1528–31.

(6) Until 1529, enforcement of the Edict of Worms was prevented through obstruction by the Lutheran states. But at the second Diet of Speyer 1529, called by the Emperor Charles V, its enforcement was made compulsory. The six Lutheran princes and fourteen of the cities signed a Protestation affirming their right to answer to God alone for what concerned 'God's honor and the salvation of the souls of each one of us.' From this they were called Protestants.

(7) The Colloquy of Marburg 1529 was an attempt to unite the various branches of the reform movement. Agreement was

---

8   Martin Luther, 'Against the Robbing and Murdering Hordes of Peasants,' in *Luther's Works: Volume 46: The Christian in Society, III* (Robert C. Schultz; 1525; repr., Philadelphia: Fortress Press, 1967), 54–55.

reached on 14 out of 15 propositions. What prevented final concord was the Lord's Supper. Luther was intransigent, insisting on the corporeal presence of the body of Christ, repeatedly underlining the word *est* (is) in Jesus' statement 'This is my body.' He opposed transubstantiation but insisted that Christ's presence was corporeal. At the end a limited agreement was signed but a permanent rift among the Reformers remained.[9]

LUTHER'S THEOLOGY

Luther became a Catholic theologian when he suddenly switched from jurisprudence to theology as the result of his experience in a severe thunderstorm. At Erfurt he was educated in the *via moderna*. However, how did he become a Protestant theologian? The issue revolved around assurance of salvation, which Luther realized was not possible in the nominalist—*via moderna*—framework, for certainty about anything was impossible on that basis, since reality was held to exist purely in particulars, ruling out certain knowledge of transcendent matters. He underwent intense and agonizing struggles of conscience, realizing that his best efforts were inadequate to find favour with God. Fortunately, this was short-lived or he would have been unable to endure it. This shaped all that followed.

Luther's lectures lasted from 1513–46. His exclusive concern here was biblical exegesis. He left systematic theology to the younger Philip Melanchthon. Luther's main focus was on the Old Testament. He was also involved in disputations and biblical translations.

His writings are filled with invective, coarse and crude. He wrote under pressure and with intense inward tension. Even for the sixteenth century the profusion of empty insults are

9   B.J. Kidd, *Documents Illustrative of the Continental Reformation* (1911; repr., Oxford: Clarendon Press, 1967), 247–55; Atkinson, *Luther*, 269–77.

astounding. Characteristic is the use of scatological language. Luther's predilection for such language would not make him a welcome guest at a dinner party, even in today's coarsened environment. Oberman describes his language as 'unfitting for any respectable home.'[10] For instance, in a sermon to members of his order on 1 May 1515 he referred to slander in these terms: 'A slanderer does nothing but ruminate the filth of others with his own teeth and wallow like a pig with his nose in the dirt. That is also why his droppings stink most, surpassed only by the devil's...and though man drops his excrements in private, the slanderer does not respect this privacy. He gluts on the pleasure of wallowing in it, and he does not deserve better according to God's righteous judgment. When the slanderer whispers: Look how he has shit on himself, the best answer is: You go eat it.'[11] This was common language in reference to the devil in monastic contexts, although it appeared crude and vulgar to others of his contemporaries. Luther was proud of it and arranged for a wide distribution of the sermon. Oberman argues that Luther's lifelong barrage of crude words was aimed at the diabolical profanation of God. He constructed 'a new language of filth' to do battle against the greatest of all slanderers.[12]

In August 1536 the Elector of Saxony decreed that the Jews be expelled from his territory. This was a not uncommon tactic at the time. Luther in general urged toleration so that they could convert to Christianity. However, he increasingly opposed them on the grounds that they blasphemed Christ. In his tract *Of the Jews and their lies* (1543) he advised the authorities to burn down synagogues, to confiscate rabbinical books and to expel those Jews who would not convert. While he allows a toleration that

10   Heiko A. Oberman, *Luther: Man Between God and the Devil* (New Haven: Yale University Press, 1989), 106.

11   Heiko A. Oberman, *Luther*, 107–8.

12   Heiko A. Oberman, *Luther*, 108–9.

leaves room for conversion, this is in effect a manual for ethnic cleansing, bitter and vile invective in almost every sentence, although he never used the inflammatory medieval attack that the Jews were the murderers of Christ.[13] In an earlier writing, in 1523, he had urged that Jewish people be treated gently; 'if we really want to help them, we must be guided in our dealings with them not by papal law but by the law of Christian love' he urged.[14] Yet the anti-semitism is clear in a way which it was equally clearly absent in other reformers.

We have about 3,000 of Luther's letters extant. He issued thirty devotional writings from 1517–20 which went through 370 impressions, some through 24 printings in three years.

His theology is marked throughout by antitheses, the most significant of which are listed below. In this, I am following the outline suggested by Gerhard Ebeling.[15]

(1) The letter and the spirit. The letter refers to knowledge based on Scripture and seen in formal doctrinal statements, and the spirit to faith and experience deriving from the Holy Spirit. The former is knowledge about the gospel, the latter is the living faith of the gospel. Luther viewed the literal sense of Scripture Christologically (so that the text of the Psalter is concerned with Christ). Thus the literal sense of Scripture is spiritual because it is Christological. This entailed the abandonment of allegory, on which much exegesis had previously relied.[16]

(2) The law and the gospel. Law means demand, while gospel refers to promise and gift. The whole of Scripture and theology depends upon distinguishing between the law and the gospel,

13   Heiko A. Oberman, *Luther*, 290–97.

14   Martin Luther, 'That Jesus Christ Was Born a Jew,' in *Luther's Works: Volume 45: The Christian in Society, II* (Brandt, Walther J.: Lehmann, Helmut T. ed, PL; 1523; repr., Philadelphia: Fortress Press, 1962), 229.

15   Gerhard Ebeling, *Luther: An Introduction to His Thought* (R.A. Wilson; London: Collins, 1972), 93–241.

16   Ebeling, *Luther*, 93–109.

Luther said.[17] This is not an antithesis, an either/or, for law is not replaced by gospel or the latter would be a new law. Luther opposed the antinomians. It is not reducible to a contrast between Old and New Testaments, for most of Luther's work was in the Old Testament. Nor is the distinction complementary, as if the law required the gospel to complete it. Nor is it a formal logical distinction that is purely theoretical. Rather, Luther viewed it in dynamic, existential terms. It is a battle in which law and gospel are mortal enemies. Where this distinction is blurred, the gospel is abandoned since the gospel is not then seen in opposition to the law. The gospel is only gospel when it is distinguished from and opposed to the law.[18] Hence many influenced by Luther can think that the Reformed are heretical, eroding the gospel by blurring the antithesis between law and gospel.[19]

For Luther, the law lays a burden on man to be borne by his own abilities, it leaves him on his own. The word of God in this sense is law and anger, in which God remains hidden. In the gospel, by contrast, God comes as one who is present. Thus, the sole purpose of the word is to evoke faith—therefore the gospel is justification through the word alone through faith alone. Yet the law and the gospel, while opposed in themselves are mutually related, for the law leads us to the gospel.[20]

(3) Twofold use of the law. The law has a theological use—it leads us to Christ. It also has a civil use—to maintain order in society by restricting the consequences of sin. Luther's position on whether the decalogue has a continuing place in the Christian life is complex. He says that the Christian has no need of the law since he is directed by the Spirit but the excesses of the

---

17   Ebeling, *Luther*, 110–11; Paul Althaus, *The Theology of Martin Luther* (Robert C. Schultz; Philadelphia: Fortress Press, 1966), 251.

18   Ebeling, *Luther*, 110–24; Althaus, *Luther*, 257–59.

19   Contrast the statement of the Westminster Confession of Faith that the law and the gospel 'sweetly comply together' (WCF 19:7).

20   Althaus, *Luther*, 260; Atkinson, *Luther*, 102–104,117–120, 129–30.

enthusiasts led him to greater caution. He still considers the decalogue has a function but only within the wider context of the totality of biblical teaching. Melanchthon was to write of the 'third use of the law,' as a rule for Christian living and this was to find acceptance in the *Formula of Concord* and Lutheranism generally but this is not explicit in Luther, although he did write a *Treatise on Good Works* as an application of the law, regarded it as still binding and strongly opposed the enthusiasts' rejection of the law.[21] Only the gospel enables us to understand the law as law, and only the theological use of the law, as it directs us to Christ, provides the rationale for the correct view of the civil use of the law.[22]

(4) Faith and love. Faith is the doer, love is the deed. Faith gives power to love, as the driving force. Faith is the highest good work. A tension exists here as well. The Christian is free, a servant of no one—yet he is a servant with a duty to everyone. There is a paradox of radical freedom and radical servitude. Love is the consequence of justification, in contrast to the scholastics (as Augustine) for whom justification is by faith working through love.[23]

(5) The kingdom of Christ and the kingdom of the world. These two intermingle but are to be distinguished. Luther had no desire to separate the two spheres (the anabaptists did that). God is the lord of both kingdoms. They both coincide and are distinguished.[24]

(6) God hidden and revealed. Luther sets the theology of the cross (*theologia crucis*), God and man in theological terms, with a contradiction between God and the world, in contrast to the theology of glory (*theologia gloria*), assuming a harmony between God and the world. Faith and reason are radically opposed, in

21   Althaus, *Luther*, 266–73; Atkinson, *Luther*, 102–4.
22   Ebeling, *Luther*, 125–40.
23   Ebeling, *Luther*, 159–74.
24   Ebeling, *Luther*, 175–91.

contrast to Aquinas. For Luther, theology is concerned with man as guilty, with God who justifies and saves. It begins with the knowledge of God by a mediator. Thus the God who is revealed is hidden in his revelation since it occurs on the cross. He is *Deus crucifixus* and *absconditus* (God crucified and hidden), an offence to reason and contrary to the way sought by the pagan world.[25] The word of God is our opponent as the word of the law, since it destroys our own righteousness before God, while as the word of the gospel it declares the sinner righteous.[26]

LEGACY

(1) Luther, governed by his particular experiences, had a preoccupation with salvation. While this was a clear focus, it seems to be a restriction. It is clear from experience that God deals differently with different people. Here, a whole movement was hijacked by the extraordinary experience of one individual. The focus on individual salvation may have prevented Luther's followers from developing the more expansive worldview common to Reformed theology.

(2) Luther, and his followers, were less militant than those of Reformed Protestantism. He and they enjoyed the protection of rulers, and after the Augsburg Interim (1548) of Empire-wide law. Luther was also more conservative politically. His soteriological preoccupation, mentioned above, fed more readily into the pietism that is evident in the language of some of the arias in Johann Sebastian Bach's *St Matthew Passion*. Hence, there was much less reflection on the political role of the church and its members, since the Lutheran church had no reason to wish for the overthrow of its patrons. In contrast, the Reformed were

25 Ebeling, *Luther*, 227–28.
26 Ebeling, *Luther*, 226–41.

almost always in a minority, frequently facing the question of whether armed resistance was to be undertaken.

(3) The law-gospel tension facilitated all of the above. It may also have encouraged long-term a lowered view of the Old Testament, feeding into higher criticism and eventually into open anti-semitism in Germany. To blame Luther for the Nazis is far-fetched and anachronistic but, notwithstanding, he was part of an anti-semitic bias that eventually was to radicalize in a frenzied policy of militant, systematic genocide. His treatise against the Jews is chillingly similar to the policies of Hitler and reflects on his perceived need to guard 'our German brothers' against what he calls the pernicious presence of the Jewish people.

(4) Many identify—wrongly—what is Protestant, and even Reformed, with Luther's sharp division between law and gospel.

(5) The one obvious legacy of Luther is Lutheranism and the Lutheran churches, although the extent to which Luther's own theology was maintained is open to question; even in the sixteenth century changes introduced by Melanchthon had a widespread impact.

(6) Having said that, Luther's achievement was obviously colossal. The Reformation occurred spontaneously throughout Europe and no one man engineered it. It was a work of the Holy Spirit. A preoccupation with Luther is one-sided. However, without Luther it is hard to see how the movement would have flourished as much as it did.

FOR FURTHER READING

Luther's Works. 55 volumes. Ed. Jaroslav Pelikan. St. Louis: Concordia Press, 1955.

Althaus, Paul. *The Theology of Martin Luther.* Robert C. Schultz. Philadelphia: Fortress Press, 1966.

Atkinson, James. *Martin Luther and the Birth of Protestantism.*
    1968. Repr.. Atlanta: John Knox Press, 1982.

Oberman, Heiko A. *Luther: Man Between God and the Devil.*
    New Haven: Yale University Press, 1989.

Oberman, Heiko Augustinus. *The Harvest of Medieval Theology:
    Gabriel Biel and Late Medieval Nominalism.* Grand Rapids:
    Eerdmans, 1967.

8

HEINRICH BULLINGER (1504–75)

LIFE

Bullinger was born on 18 July 1504 at Bremgarten, the youngest of five sons. His father was the parish priest and was not formally married until 31 December 1529 in a ceremony at the cathedral in Zurich. During his childhood Heinrich experienced a number of remarkable deliverances from death. He recovered from the plague by the skin of his teeth. On another occasion he fell in the street and a whistle he was carrying was driven into his neck. He also narrowly escaped abduction. After attending Latin school, he went to Emmerich, on the Rhine, in 1516 with a brother to continue his education. He rapidly advanced in Latin but had to beg for a living by singing door-to-door. His father had restricted his income so as to teach him moderation and also to engender sympathy for the poor. This was not uncongenial to Heinrich, who wanted to join the Carthusians, the strictest order of monks. In 1519 he enrolled at the University of Cologne. He received a bachelor's degree in 1520 and a master's in 1522. During this time he studied Peter Lombard, and followed up Lombard's frequent citations of the Fathers by reading them himself. He gained access to a Dominican library and read Chrysostom, Ambrose, Origen and Augustine, as well as the early Luther and a copy of the New Testament. Through this, as one of his biographers remarks, 'Bullinger's mind and heart opened gradually to the knowledge and reception of the gospel in its purity.'[1] In 1522 the burning of Luther's books aroused in him an increased interest in theology. He returned to his father's house at Bremgarten and devoted himself to a study of the Bible, with the aid of Athanasius and Cyprian. He also devoured Luther's treatises. By this time he had come to evangelical views.

In January 1523, at the age of eighteen, he accepted the position of head teacher at the Cistercian monastery at Kappel. The good news was that he did not have to make any monastic vows to do so. He lectured on Scripture with the aid of the Fathers, Erasmus and Melanchthon. He wrote Latin commentaries on most of the books of the NT. Through his work, the monastery itself was reformed. In September 1525 the mass was abolished and the Reformed eucharist introduced the following March. He met Huldrych Zwingli in 1523 and was influenced by Zwingli's views on the Lord's Supper. In 1525 he attended the first disputation with the anabaptists in Zurich and acted as clerk at the second and third disputations in March. For five months in 1527 he had a leave of absence to attend Zwingli's lectures in Zurich, during which time he devoted himself to a study of Greek and Hebrew texts. In January 1528 he accompanied Zwingli to the Berne disputation and met other Swiss reformers there.

In May 1529 he left the monastery to succeed his father as pastor at Bremgarten. By the end of June Bremgarten had

---

1   Henry Bullinger, *The Fifth Decade* (Volume Four of *The Decades of Henry Bullinger, Minister of the Church in Zurich*; for the Parker Society by the Rev. Thomas Harding; 1550–51; repr., Cambridge: At the University Press, 1852), viii.

become a Reformed town. In August he married an ex-nun, Anna Adlischwyler. Then in 1531 Zwingli was killed in battle. Bullinger was forced to flee to Zurich at this time, arriving on 21 November. On 13 December he accepted an invitation to succeed Zwingli as Antistes of the Zurich church. He was to remain in that position until his death almost 44 years later. After his first sermon in Zurich cathedral, Myconius wrote that many thought Zwingli was not dead at all but had come back to life like the phoenix.[2] Bullinger had eleven children, six sons and five daughters, plus a virtual adopted son, Rudolf Gwalther, who joined the household in 1532 aged 13, and succeeded Bullinger on his death in 1575, and was by this time his son-in-law. Many students lived in his house over the years, as did his own parents. He also cared for Zwingli's survivors.

HIS WORK IN ZURICH

Bullinger's first task in Zurich was to preserve the Reformation there. Rumours circulated that Zurich was to revert to Rome. Many in the city favoured that direction. Bullinger drafted a mandate in May 1532 reaffirming Zurich's commitment to the Reformed faith and renewing all the legislation on morals enacted during the time of Zwingli. Later in 1532 he and Leo Jud reorganized and enlarged the scope of the Synod. In particular this mandate provided for supervision of the selection, lives and morals of the clergy and required them to take an annual oath of allegiance to Zurich. Additionally, officers of the city council were made members of the Synod. Thus the church was placed firmly under the control of the civil authority. The task of the clergy was simply to preach and to perform their pastoral duties. However, Bullinger had the task—and opportunity—of regular orations to the council, instructing it where it disagreed with the

2   Ibid., xi.

church leaders. Much of the relationship between church and state revolved around Bullinger himself and the cordial relations he was able to maintain with the leading civic dignitaries.

Until 1538 Bullinger's

> preachings were daily, sometimes twice on the day; his publications...
> were voluminous...his pastoral and synodical, civil and ecclesiastical
> engagements were unceasing and very various; his correspondence
> was exceedingly extensive and critical; and his house was always
> open...ready to shelter and befriend especially refugees from
> every country where religious persecution raged. And during the
> protracted efforts to effect a reconciliation between the Lutherans
> and the church of Zurich on the sacramentarian question, his
> moderation and sincerity were eminently conspicuous.[3]

In 1542 his preaching activity was reduced to two sermons, on Friday and Sunday. He directed the Zurich academy until 1537, from when he continued as professor of theology. In 1536 he assisted in producing the *First Helvetic Confession*.

Bullinger had an impact way beyond Zurich. He was an amazingly prolific correspondent. There are 9,500 letters extant from Luther, Zwingli, and Calvin combined but as many as 12,000 from Bullinger alone. He corresponded with leading French Protestants, and with Protestants in Poland and Hungary. He received exiles from Germany when Reformed cities in the south were re-Catholicized. He had French exiles in his house from time to time. However, it is particularly with English reformers that his connections were strong. John Hooper and his wife stayed in his home from 1547–9. Hooper returned to become Bishop of Gloucester and Bullinger became godfather of Hooper's daughter. Then, after Queen Mary came to the throne in 1553, a flood of exiles poured into Zurich. In contrast to the Genevan exiles, most of these achieved high office in the Church of England after Elizabeth acceded following the death

---

3   Ibid., xii.

of Bloody Mary. These included Robert Beaumont (later Vice-Chancellor of Cambridge University), Thomas Bentham (Bishop of Coventry and Lichfield), William Cole (Dean of Lincoln), Robert Horn (Bishop of Winchester), Laurence Humphrey (Dean of Winchester), John Jewel (Bishop of Salisbury), Roger Kelke (Archdeacon of Stowe), Thomas Lever (Canon of Durham), John Mullins (Archdeacon of London), John Parkhurst (Bishop of Norwich), James Pilkington (Bishop of Durham), Michael Reniger (Archdeacon of Winchester), Francis Russell (Earl of Bedford), Edwin Sandys (Archbishop of York), Thomas Spencer (Archdeacon of Chichester) and John Aylmer (Bishop of London).[4] In 1577 John Whitgift, Dean of Lincoln, made Bullinger's Decades (a series of fifty sermons arranged into five groups of ten, preached between 1549–51, containing a comprehensive discussion of Christian doctrine) required reading for all clergy in the diocese. Nine years later, following his appointment as Archbishop of Canterbury, he repeated the measure for all unqualified clergy, requiring them to read one of the sermons every week and to be examined on such reading once per quarter.[5]

Bullinger is the author of the *Second Helvetic Confession* (1566). This is a comprehensive statement of the Reformed faith. It was very soon accepted by the Reformed churches in Switzerland except for Basel, Germany, France and eastern Europe. It also had an extensive influence in England, Scotland and the Netherlands. It remains the single most widely accepted confession in the Reformed tradition. When he died, after a long illness, Bullinger's remains were deposited in Zurich cathedral 'amid the sincere and lively regrets of all classes of his townspeople.'[6]

4   See David J. Keep, 'Henry Bullinger and the Elizabethan Church,' PhD thesis (University of Sheffield, 1970), 52.

5   Keep, 'Bulllinger,' 106–24.

6   Henry Bullinger, *The Fifth Decade*, xiv.

HIS THEOLOGY

While Bullinger came to evangelical convictions in part through reading Luther, he can in no way be described as a follower of Luther. The most characteristic features of Luther's theology are absent from Bullinger, while Bullinger's most prominent interests are alien to Luther. Moreover, he is distinctively different from Zwingli. By the time Calvin appeared on the scene Bullinger was a comparatively old hand as a reformer and, while there is some evidence that Calvin may have had an impact on Bullinger later in the latter's career, all the pointers are that he was his own man and developed a distinctive theology of his own. In what follows we will highlight some of its main features.

In contrast to Luther

As we remarked in chapter 7, justification by faith was right at the centre of Luther's theology. It became the critical test of true doctrine for Luther's followers. This was not the case with Zwingli, nor was it with Bullinger. Both believed in justification by faith, of that there is no doubt. However, they did not give it the same significance as Luther did.

Again, Luther held to a sharp contrast between the law and the gospel. This pervaded his theology and affected the way he read the Bible. It is one of the factors behind his rejection of the Letter of James, since he considered it lacked the gospel and emphasized the law. Bullinger, on the other hand, saw law and gospel in continuum rather than contrast. This came to expression in his views on the covenant of grace, as we shall see in a moment.

Luther also had a very strong doctrine of predestination. This he shared with Zwingli. However, Bullinger taught a much milder form of predestination and there is very little evidence that he held to double predestination, although later in his career he appears to move in that direction.

One other matter needs to be mentioned. Luther taught that in the Eucharist the body and blood of Christ are present in a carnal, corporeal manner. In contrast to Rome, the bread and wine do not undergo a change of substance and become the body and blood of Christ. However, the body and blood of Christ are present. At the Colloquy of Marburg in 1529 Luther repeatedly wrote on the table in chalk 'this is my body' underlining the word 'is.' He vehemently opposed Zwingli's idea, which Bullinger shared, that the verb is to be understood as 'represents.' In contrast, Bullinger did not believe that the body and blood of Christ were corporeally present in the sacrament.

Covenant theology

Zwingli was the first to argue, in 1525, that infants should be baptized on the grounds of the unity of the covenant of grace. Bullinger accepted this argument. He wrote the first treatise devoted specifically to God's covenant, *De testamento seu foedere Dei unco et aeterno* (1534). It was reprinted as an appendix to five different editions of his New Testament commentaries (from 1537–58). His argument here is found also in many others of his works. The treatise was directed against the anabaptist denial of the continued validity of the OT. The theme of covenant unity throughout the history of redemption had already surfaced in Zwingli and Oecolampadius. However, Bullinger introduced nuances not present before. Bullinger's definition of terms is important. He realizes the Greek word *diatheke* can be used either for a testament and a promise, or for a bargain or agreement. Where it refers to a promise it is always confirmed by an oath, but otherwise he considers that it means a pact, which best translates the Hebrew *berith* used by Moses in Genesis 15 and 17. Bullinger uses the latter to define covenant.[7] Both Zwingli

7   Heinrich Bullinger, *De Testamento Seu Foedere Dei Unico & Aeterno Brevis Expositio* (Zürich, 1534), 4.

and Oecolampadius, recognizing the presence of both ideas, had favoured testament as best expressing the concept of covenant in the Bible.[8] Bullinger departs from this. He proceeds to expand his definitions of *testamentum* and of *pactum* or *foedus*. Certain conditions are placed on the parties in the pact of friendship. The basic idea is a mutually established agreement. God has established the covenant with miserable, sinful man out of mere grace, but the pattern throughout is mutuality. Both God and man agree to observe the conditions, and the words of Moses recording the covenant (or, indeed, the whole canon of Scripture) transmit the covenant terms to posterity.[9] The decalogue is a paraphrase of the covenantal conditions.[10] In his polemic against the anabaptists, Bullinger sees infant baptism as a condition of the covenant as crucial as circumcision. The anabaptists neglect the promise of God by excluding children of believing parents from the covenant conditions.[11]

In considering the covenantal conditions, Bullinger again presents a mutual compact. We know clearly what God demands of us and what we may expect from him. He has revealed his nature in the covenant and shows what he requires of us. The corollary is entailed—if we obey the conditions, we may expect the promises. Our part in the covenant and the way we can fulfil the conditions is by clinging to God constantly through faith and by pleasing him with a holy life.[12] Bullinger proceeds to talk of God promising to protect his people, to liberate them from sin and eternal death and to grant them eternal life,[13] of Christ

---

8   Robert W. A. Letham, 'Faith and Assurance in Reformed Theology: Zwingli to the Synod of Dort: 2 Vols,' PhD thesis (University of Aberdeen, 1979), 1:45–46.

9   Heinrich Bullinger, *De Testamento*, 4–6.

10   Ibid., 19.

11   Ibid., 9–10.

12   Ibid., 12–16.

13   Ibid., 14.

fulfilling the covenant in that his death and resurrection are certain testimonies of divine mercy, by which God sets before our eyes his promise to bless us and to receive us into his fellowship and the eternal kingdom.[14] However, his previous definitions and the resulting emphases mean this element of promise and fulfilment is only part of the covenant, the whole of which is reciprocal and conditional. These promises all depend on our fulfilling the conditions. Thus, we have the threat hanging over us of excision from the covenant if we neglect the sacraments. The dedication of the *foedus* with blood signifies that an eternal curse comes on those who neglect the prescribed stipulations.[15] His view of the covenant differed in certain ways from Zwingli. Whereas they both had a strong emphasis on the sovereignty of God's promise and saw the covenant as fulfilled for us by Christ, Bullinger considered God's promise to be conditional and so requires fulfilment by ourselves. God promises to be gracious to those who keep the covenant conditions, while Zwingli and Calvin (together with Bucer and Vermigli) pointed to Christ as having fulfilled those conditions for us and saw our part in terms of obligations of gratitude.[16]

Bullinger's view of the covenant has obvious implications for assurance of salvation. Not surprisingly he differs here from Calvin and the others too. Clearly, he considers faith as a condition of the covenant.[17] He does not reflect on the origins of faith, except for stating that God saves us.[18] Since he stresses covenant unity, he insists the faith of Adam, Abraham, Moses, David and Paul was one. Faith is personal, directed to God, Christ or God's promise.[19]

14   Ibid., 22.
15   Ibid., 42.
16   Ibid., 14–22.
17   Ibid., 5, 16, 23f, 42f.
18   Ibid., 5.
19   Ibid., 23f.

Thus it is active, as trust, clinging to God, or following Christ.[20] While by faith we believe that God is good, just and beneficent,[21] nowhere does Bullinger go further and say that faith is equivalent to assurance of salvation, apart from possibly once.[22] Note that for Calvin, saving faith is assurance of salvation (*Institute* 3:2:7). Bullinger's stress on covenant conditions encourages him to view faith as active trust in fulfilment of these conditions. Assurance could only be present once we fulfil the conditions. Election is conspicuous by its absence and thus Bullinger's focus is on our side of the covenant. This despite Bierma's claim that 'Bullinger places a good deal of emphasis on the unilateral divine promise of the covenant', for which he provides no references.[23]

Bullinger maintains there is only one covenant, from Adam to the present. The idea of a pre-fall covenant was not to surface until 1585. Thus this covenant is the same in substance in both OT and NT. His argument is that in the OT the covenant sign was circumcision, while in the NT the covenant sign is baptism. Since male infants received the covenant sign in the OT, infants are to be baptized in the NT. Thus the NT interprets the OT and both are in continuity. Hence, for Bullinger the covenant supports the baptism of infants. Infants are to be baptized since they are in the covenant due to the promise of God. This argument was to be developed and refined later by Calvin, Martin Bucer, and Peter Martyr Vermigli.[24] Since they had a stronger doctrine of election than Bullinger they were able more consistently to point to the promise of God as the basis for baptism. Bullinger's weak doctrine of election is his achilles heel here, for the centre

20   Ibid., 23.

21   Ibid., 24.

22   Ibid., 12.

23   Lyle D. Bierma, *German Calvinism in the Confessional Age: The Covenant Theology of Caspar Olevianus* (Grand Rapids: Baker Books, 1996), 37.

24   Robert Letham, 'Baptism in the Writings of the Reformers,' *SBET* 7, no. 2 (Autumn 1989): 21–44.

of gravity becomes our response to the covenant conditions rather than what God has done for us in grace. One point worth noting is that Bullinger, as they, held that immersion is the most appropriate mode of baptism, although sprinkling is legitimate.[25]

Bullinger also argued from the covenant for the authority of the civil magistrate over the church. Along the lines of his previous commitment to the unity of the one covenant of grace, he saw the pattern for the Christian community in the OT. The pastor is the successor of the prophets and the magistrate succeeds the kings. Therefore, the magistrate alone, as the kings in the OT, has the authority to establish religion and discipline the Christian community. The task of the pastor is to preach the word of God. Thus there is for Bullinger only one sphere, while the magistrate and pastor are distinguished by their respective tasks within that sphere.[26]

The Lord's Supper
Bullinger was strongly influenced by Zwingli on the Eucharist. However, he viewed it as more than a memorial and so his position was not precisely identical to his predecessor's. For Bullinger, the Supper is a testimony of God's grace. This is different from Calvin's doctrine, for whom the Supper is an instrument of God's grace. For Calvin, Christ is given in the Lord's Supper while for Bullinger the sacrament points to grace that is available elsewhere.[27] The two did, however, reach an agreement of sorts on the subject. The *Consensus Tigurinus* (1549) was as much a political document as anything. Calvin made major concessions to secure this agreement in the face of the problems created by the Augsburg Interim of 1548, which had parcelled up Europe

25   Ibid; Henry Bullinger, *The Fifth Decade*, 328–32, 352, 364–65.

26   J. Wayne Baker, *Heinrich Bullinger and the Covenant: The Other Reformed Tradition* (Athens, Ohio: Ohio University Press, 1980), 117–40.

27   See B.A. Gerrish, *Grace and Gratitude: The Eucharistic Theology of John Calvin* (Minneapolis: Fortress Press, 1993).

between Catholic and Lutheran jurisdictions, leaving the Reformed out in the cold. The need of the hour was for a united front in the face of a threatening political situation.[28]

Bullinger's views on the Eucharist are again connected with his theology of the covenant. The Eucharist is a symbol of God's promise of redemption to those who were in the covenant by virtue of baptism. We recall that his idea of the covenant as a mutual compact puts the weight on our human response to the conditions God has laid down for us to fulfill. For Calvin, in contrast, the covenant testifies to what God has already done for us in Christ. Differences on the Lord's Supper reflect underlying theological differences. Thus Bullinger defended Zwingli's view of the Lord's Supper against both Catholics and Luther in 1532. He also opposed the Wittenburg Concord of 1536—an attempt by Bucer to effect a compromise between Luther and the Swiss (Bucer had a profound impact on Calvin).

Predestination
Whereas Zwingli had a powerful doctrine of election and predestination,[29] and Calvin clearly taught and defended double predestination (both election and reprobation), Bullinger's was a much less robust and developed predestinarianism. He wanted to preserve a stress on God's freedom and grace but he was also interested in God's goodness and our human responsibility. Bullinger was a preacher more than a theologian and definitely not a systematic thinker. Venema correctly assesses the situation

28   Paul E. Rorem, 'The Consensus Tigurinus (1549): Did Calvin Compromise?' in *Calvinus Sacrae Scripturae Professor: Calvin as Confessor of Holy Scripture: Die Referate Des Congrès International Des Recherches Calviniennees Vom 20. Bis 23. August 1990 in Grand Rapids* (Wilhelm H. Neuser; Grand Rapids: Eerdmans, 1994), 72–90.

29   W.P. Stephens, *The Theology of Huldrych Zwingli* (Oxford: Clarendon Press, 1986), 97–107; Robert W. A. Letham, 'Faith and Assurance,' 1:17–22, 2:7–10.

by affirming Bullinger's acceptance of Reformed doctrine, that the elect and reprobate are not distinguished merely by the fact that the former trust Christ and the latter do not, but rather on the basis of God's sovereign electing purpose. However, his interest was mainly on the preaching of God's promises.[30]

However, as his career proceeded, there is evidence that he was prepared to be more explicit when the need arose. In his Decades he clearly teaches double predestination.[31] He does so implicitly in the *Second Helvetic Confession* where he also uses the language of Calvin, from his *Institute* 3:24:4–5.[32] However, it is hard to find clear evidence beyond this that he accepted reprobation. At the start of the Arminian controversy in the Netherlands in the last decade of the century, his name was frequently used by

30   See Cornelis P. Venema, *Heinrich Bullinger and the Doctrine of Predestination: Author of 'the Other Reformed Tradition?* (Grand Rapids: Baker, 2002), 113–20.

31   'And the predestination of God is the eternal decree of God, whereby he hath ordained either to save or to destroy men; a most certain end of life and death being appointed unto them.' Henry Bullinger, *The Fourth Decade* (Volume 3 of *The Decades of Henry Bullinger, Minister of the Church of Zurich*; for the Parker Society by the Revd Thomas Harding; 1550–51; repr., Cambridge: At the University Press, 1851), 185 Also, 'God by his eternal and unchangeable counsel hath foreappointed who are to be saved, and who are to be condemned. Now the end or [sic] the decree of life and death is short and manifest to all the godly.' Ibid., 186. See also, Ibid., 187.

32   'We therefore condemn those who seek otherwise than in Christ whether they be chosen from all eternity, and what God has decreed of them before all beginning. For men must hear the Gospel preached, and believe it. If thou believest, and art in Christ, thou mayest undoubtedly hold that thou art elected. For the Father has revealed unto us in Christ his eternal sentence of predestination' (X,7–8). 'Let Christ, therefore, be our looking-glass, in whom we may behold our predestination. We shall have a most evident and sure testimony that we are written in the Book of Life if we communicate with Christ, and he be ours, and we be his, by a true faith. Let this comfort us in the temptation touching predestination, than which there is none more dangerous, that the promises of God are general to the faithful' (X,9). Philip Schaff, *The Creeds of Christendom* (Grand Rapids: Baker, 1966), 3:848–49. Cf., John Calvin, *Institute*, 3:24:4–5.

the precursors of Arminius in support of their departure from Reformed orthodoxy. However, Venema has undermined the claim that Bullinger's theology could in any way be compatible with the supporters of Arminius.[33]

Church and state

For Bullinger, the church is under the authority of the civil (Christian) magistrate. He was arguing strongly against the anabaptists, who radically separated church and state into two separate spheres, and argued against Christians taking oaths in court or serving in the army.

We should note the congruity of this view with the situation of the English church. This helps to explain the corresponding influence Bullinger had with the English churchmen who fled in exile to Zurich during the reign of Queen Mary (1553–8), many of whom who later achieved high office. At this point, Bullinger and Calvin diverged. Calvin held that there were two distinct spheres of governmental authority, with the church having control over church discipline. It is significant that few of the Marian exiles who went to Geneva held high office in the Church of England under Elizabeth. Edmund Grindal is the one exception, becoming Archbishop of Canterbury, but a poor one who did not command wide support. Calvin's view of church-state relations hardly appealed to a Queen who wanted to maintain her powers. In this case, power held by the church authorities was something of a challenge. Furthermore, John Knox—who had spent time in Geneva during the Marian exile—made matters worse by his *First Blast of the Trumpet against the Monstrous Regiment of Women*, in which he denounced female rulers. While this was aimed mainly at Queen Mary, with a sideways glance at Mary, Queen of Scots, Elizabeth unsurprisingly took it badly.

---

33   Venema, *Bullinger*, 47–50, 114–20.

SUMMARY

Bullinger is not the most prominent of the Reformers in the minds of the Christian public, nor was he the most creative of theologians. However, his influence was extensive. This was due to his warm personality and extensive network of contacts. His voluminous letter writing, together with the hospitality he showed to exiles from other places gave him a voice far greater than others. The one exception to his lack of theological innovation was his role in the emergence of covenant theology which, in turn, was to have a far-reaching impact in generations to come.

FOR FURTHER READING

Bullinger, Henry. *The Decades of Henry Bullinger, Minister of the Church in Zurich*. 4 vols. For the Parker Society by the Rev. Thomas Harding. 1550–51. Cambridge: At the University Press, 1849–52.

Gerrish, B.A. Grace and Gratitude: *The Eucharistic Theology of John Calvin*. Minneapolis: Fortress Press, 1993.

Keep, David J. 'Henry Bullinger and the Elizabethan Church.' PhD thesis. University of Sheffield, 1970.

Letham, Robert. 'Baptism in the Writings of the Reformers.' SBET 7, no. 2 (Autumn 1989): 21–44.

Rorem, Paul E. 'The Consensus Tigurinus (1549): Did Calvin Compromise?' *In Calvinus Sacrae Scripturae Professor: Calvin as Confessor of Holy Scripture*: Die Referate Des Congrès International Des Recherches Calviniennees Vom 20. Bis 23. August 1990 in Grand Rapids, Wilhelm H. Neuser, 72–90. Grand Rapids: Eerdmans, 1994.

Venema, Cornelis P. *Heinrich Bullinger and the Doctrine of Predestination: Author of 'the Other Reformed Tradition'?* Grand Rapids: Baker, 2002.

9

JOHN CALVIN (1509–64)

LIFE

Born on 10 July 1509 in Noyon, in Picardy, Calvin's father, a burgher, was a trustee for the cathedral chapter in Noyon. John and his elder brother received church benefices to provide for their study of theology. From 1523 Calvin studied at the Collège de la Marche in Paris, and then liberal arts at the Collège Montaigu. After his father fell out with the cathedral authorities he urged his son to abandon theology, so he went to Orleans to study law. This way he avoided being dominated by the speculative scholasticism of late medieval theology.

Calvin returned to Paris later to study at the Collège Royal, where the influence of the humanists Erasmus and Lefevre d'Etaples was strong. This was in contrast to the Sorbonne which was arch-conservative and connected with the Inquisition. Here, in Paris in 1532, he published his first work a commentary on Seneca's De Clementia. He began to associate with a group that read both Erasmus and Luther. He was known by his friends as the accusative case. He was irascible—a lifelong trait—and didn't suffer fools gladly.

When did Calvin become a Protestant? What is the date of his conversion? That is not entirely clear and it is a question that has engendered much debate among Calvin scholars. Completely unlike Luther, Calvin was a very private person and wrote little about himself. He wrote later that it happened 'suddenly' (*subito*). God surprised him by a sudden conversion which consisted in subduing his heart and making it teachable.[1] There were none of the agonies experienced by Luther. We have sixteen letters extant from 1530–34 when he was in France.

His Seneca commentary shows no sign of Protestant influence. In it he seems intent on making a career for himself as a man of letters. There is not the slightest trace of personal involvement in connection with the treatise. Until 1533 we have no information on his religious convictions, if he had any. In June 1533, he writes to François Daniel an account of his conversation with Daniel's sister, Claudine, about the vows she was to take in the Abbey of La Saussaye. He doubts that her decision is a mature one. But there is no hint that he is opposed to perpetual vows. Later in 1533, on All Saints' Day, his friend Nicholas Cop, who had surprisingly become Rector of the University of Paris, gave his famous rectorial address on the Sermon on the Mount and justification by faith. This caused a furore. The Inquisition stepped in. It has been thought that the speech was composed by Calvin. However, Calvin wrote a circular letter at the time giving an account of these events in an ironic tone, treating both the theologians of the Sorbonne and Cop alike. Although he shows a good knowledge of the questions raised by the supporters of Erasmus and Luther, he is equally clearly an outsider. However, since he was identified by the authorities with Cop, he was forced to flee for his life. In

---

1   Calvin's preface to his commentary on the Psalms: *CO*, 31:22.

another letter, undated but probably written early in 1534, he says he is no longer in Paris, is studying, supported by a patron, but is unable to study peacefully, but nevertheless he is in God's hands. This does not require Reformation belief but it could indicate that he had moved to acceptance of it. Certainly, by 4 May 1534 he had given up all his benefices.

Calvin anticipated a life of study and aimed to reach Strassburg, where the Reformation had been long established under the leadership of Martin Bucer. In 1536, on the way there, he stopped at Geneva, where Guillaume Farel had preached the evangelical faith for four years without affecting the structure of the church. There Farel ordered him to stay, with dire threats should he desist. He took the title of lecturer in holy Scripture. He and Farel attempted to reform the church, publishing a church ordinance, a catechism, and a confession of faith. In particular, in the same year Calvin produced a volume entitled *Christianae religionis institutio,* designed as instruction for the godly in the Christian religion and dedicated to King Francis I as an apologetic for the Protestants in France, Calvin insisted that the 'pious' have no intention of overthrowing the royal authority. Many subsequent editions followed in French and Latin. On 23 April 1538 Calvin and Farel were expelled from Geneva by the city council.

Calvin went to Strassburg, as he had originally intended, leading the French-speaking congregation, and remaining there until 1541. This was vital for his development. The Reformation there was in full swing under Martin Bucer. Bucer's massive commentary on Romans had already been published in 1536.[2] He was to be a big influence on Calvin all round—on election, faith, the church and sacraments. Some have argued that Calvin is a Buceran. In Strassburg, Calvin published an expanded and significantly modified version of the *Institutio*, which was to be the basis for all subsequent editions. He participated in a range

2   Martin Bucer, *In Epistolam D. Pauli Ad Romanos* (1536; repr., Basel, 1562).

of religious dialogues, with Lutherans such as Melanchthon and with Roman Catholics. The Colloquy of Regensburg (1541) is the most notable. There Bucer and Melanchthon reached agreement with Cardinals Contarini and Gropper and also with Eck, Luther's erstwhile opponent, on a wide range of doctrinal matters, including justification by faith. However, the Roman representatives were effectively blackballed on their return from the Colloquy and the accord never took root.

In turn, Cardinal Jacopo Sadoleto admonished Geneva to return to Rome. Some of Calvin's supporters in Geneva urged him to respond. This he did, saying the church was based on the word of God not tradition but that he and his friends were not introducing novelties but returning the church to its former state. This made a deep impression in Geneva and he (but not Farel) was recalled in 1541. There he remained till his death in 1564. During this time he married Idelette de Bure, a widow of an ex-anabaptist, and became the father of one son. Sadly, both wife and son predeceased him.

From 1541 until 1555 Calvin was engaged in a battle to secure the reformation as he envisaged it, with the reform of the church his great priority. His church ordinance and order of worship of 1541 lay the groundwork.[3] His structure of four offices, based on the Strassburg model, he put into effect: pastors (responsible for the ministry of the Word and sacraments, gathered together in a company of pastors), teachers (whose task was the instruction of school pupils, catechumens, and theological students), elders (selected by the city council, overseeing the conduct of members of the congregation, and forming together with the pastors the consistory), and deacons (engaged in ministry and distribution to the needy, distributing the bread and wine during the

---

3   *Calvin: Theological Treatises* (J.K.S. Reid; Philadelphia: Westminster Press, 1954), 56–72.

communion service),[4] an office Calvin single-handedly revived after more than a millennium of disuse and misuse.[5]

It was not until 1555 that his position was secure. Even then there was opposition from a faction led by Ami Perrin, a powerful figure on the city council, because of resentment at the regulation of conduct by the consistory and what was regarded as rule by foreigners—Calvin as a Frenchman was an outsider as Genevans saw it. This was not theological opposition, of which by that time there was none. Calvin was not even a citizen of Geneva until 1559. Many French Protestant refugees fled to Geneva as a haven. As in any situation where there are large numbers of immigrants, still more in the cramped confines of a small city-state, this became a source of tension with the local population until their numbers grew so great that they could no longer be discounted. Added to this, Geneva felt itself in a precarious position in its own right, subject to threat from the nearby Catholic cantons.

Calvin's final years were marked by a plethora of painful illnesses. At his wish he was buried in an unmarked grave at an unknown place with no witnesses or ceremony, since he was convinced that the glory of God should not be challenged by the honouring of people.

HIS WORK

Preaching was the main aspect of Calvin's work. Throughout the years in Geneva he preached twice each Sunday and daily every other week.[6] He arranged a rotational and collegial ministry in

---

4   John Calvin, *Institute*, 4:3:4–9.

5   Elsie Anne McKee, *John Calvin on the Diaconate and Liturgical Almsgiving* (Geneva: Librairie Droz, 1984); Jeannine Olson, *Calvin and Social Welfare: Deacons and the Bourse Franc*aise* (Selinsgrove, Pennsylvania: Susquehanna University Press, 1989).

6   T.H.L. Parker, *Calvin's Preaching* (Louisville, Kentucky: Westminster John Knox Press, 1992), 62.

Geneva. Calvin's practice was a *lectio continua*, a continuous biblical exposition proceeding through various books of the Bible and applying their teaching to his congregation. His sermons are being republished gradually. Delivered in French, they present a slightly different perspective than his commentaries and treatises.

Calvin's commentaries contain detailed interaction with the biblical text. Here Calvin is more prepared to discuss a variety of readings and interpretations. The commentaries have been translated into English many times, the edition edited by T.F. Torrance and D.W. Torrance being the standard translation of the New Testament commentaries.

The *Institute* should be read in conjunction with the commentaries. Calvin himself says so in his preface to the 1559 edition.[7] Where Calvin makes a biblical citation, it is often a shorthand sign that the reader should consult the relevant place in his commentary on that passage. The first edition of the Institute in 1536 was catechetical, aiming to teach all Christians the basics of correct belief. It was based on two of Luther's catechisms. From 1539 the work changed its scope, designed now to teach aspiring theologians.

The theological treatises deal with major controversies. Calvin's letters are many, several volumes in translation, more being rediscovered all the time. His pastoral work was focused in his role as moderator of the Company of Pastors, which was an annual appointment and made against his will, and in the consistory, which was a disciplinary body, although its discipline was predominantly pastoral.

Calvin produced a liturgy for Geneva, encouraged the translation and metrification of the psalms, translated by Clément

---

7   John Calvin, *Institutes of the Christian Religion* (John T. McNeill; ed. Ford Lewis Battles; Philadelphia: Westminster Press, 1960), 1:4–5; Elsie Anne McKee, 'Exegesis, Theology, and Development in Calvin's Institutio: A Methodological Suggestion,' in *Probing the Reformed Tradition* (Elsie Anne McKee; Louisville, Kentucky: Westminster John Knox Press, 1989), 154–72.

Marot, with music by Claude Goudimel. Calvin's views on music were positive,[8] Goudimel writing many motets setting the psalms to music for situations other than church worship. No one once listening to them can ever again say that Calvin was opposed to music.

Exiles flocked to Geneva not only from France but from persecution in England during the reign of Queen Mary (1553–8), including John Knox. Most of the Genevan exiles from England formed the Puritan party shortly after their return. Students came to Geneva from all over Europe.

Geneva

Church and state in Geneva were inter-linked, as was customary at the time. Civil rule was through a number of councils. The church was governed by the Company of Pastors, functioning rather like a presbytery. Catechetical instruction was mandated by 1545, although many and varied were the attempts to evade it by the catechumens! The consistory was responsible for discipline, although it functioned more like a counseling service, resolving marital and family disputes a good deal of the time. A team of scholars under the leadership of the late Robert M. Kingdon has transcribed the records of the consistory from badly handwritten copies.[9] The consistory was a semi-judicial tribunal (comprising all ordained pastors in Geneva, a group of elected lay elders, chaired by one of the syndics or magistrates, assisted by a secretary and a summoner). It met once a week on Thursdays. Calvin attended almost all its sessions, personally administering the admonitions. It had the power to excommunicate. This was a significant development from other Protestant cities, where

8   Charles Garside, 'Calvin's Preface to the Psalter: A Reappraisal,' *The Musical Quarterly* 38 (1951): 566–77.

9   For instance, Isabella M. Watt, *Registers of the Consistory of Geneva at the Time of Calvin: Volume 1: 1542–1544* (Grand Rapids: Eerdmans, 2002).

church discipline was in the hands of the civil magistrate. Calvin established the Genevan Academy in 1558, Theodore Beza being called as Professor of Greek and eventually Rector and Professor of Theology. Literacy became the norm.

Calvin's final years, from 1555, were focused on two main areas apart from his regular round of preaching. One of these activities was the teaching of theologians through his publications such as the *Institute*, commentaries, sermons, and the Academy. The other dominant interest was the evangelization of France, which began in 1555, went into full swing in 1558, and reached a climax in 1561. At this time persecution was on the wane, and so there was a window to win converts. In 1561 negotiations between Catholic and Protestant leaders took place at Poissy, sponsored by the government. Beza was sent there. A royal edict in 1562 proclaimed partial toleration. Calvin had welcomed thousands of French Protestant refugees into Geneva over the years in preparation for this. Many of the preachers he sent into France were from the nobility, which was vital for the triumph of Protestantism in a land ruled by the aristocracy. They came very close to general success in 1562 and 1563.[10] Perhaps if they had consented to a Lutheran understanding of the Lord's Supper, suggested by the Cardinal of Lorraine, an agreement could have been reached in which a Gallican church could have emerged, rather like the Anglican. But Calvin was so close to triumph that he declined to make such a compromise and soon events moved the other way.

Controversies

Calvin's career was marked by a range of controversies. First of all, a pastor Peter Caroli in 1536–7 developed Arian views,

10   Robert M. Kingdon, *Geneva and the Consolidation of the French Protestant Movement 1564–1572: A Contribution to the History of Congregationalism, Presbyterianism, and Calvinist Resistance Theory* (Geneva: Librairie Droz, 1967).

later defecting to Rome. In the course of this conflict, Caroli insisted that Calvin publicly announce his agreement with the Nicene creed (which Caroli opposed). This Calvin refused, on the ground that he was not going to let as wayward a figure as Caroli dictate to him what he must do. The problem for Calvin was that he was held under suspicion afterwards, particularly by Roman Catholics, for holding Arian views himself due to his refusal to support the Nicene creed on this occasion. The incident has also been used by some to claim the support of Calvin for their own untenable opinion that he held to a different form of trinitarianism than the classic Nicene version.[11]

Second, Jerome Bolsec in 1550–51 opposed Calvin's doctrine of double predestination, eventually being banished from Geneva. While Calvin was supported by Beza, other figures in the reformation like Heinrich Bullinger gave at best equivocal help.

Thirdly, a range of anti-trinitarians appeared on the scene in the 1550s, mainly Italians, such as the doctor Michael Servetus, George Blandrata, and Valentine Gentilis. These were opposed by Rome and Protestants alike but were particularly virulent towards Calvin. Servetus, under sentence of death throughout Europe, turned up one day in Geneva and was arrested. Calvin gave him time to repent of his views but he refused. The city council insisted he should be burned, although Calvin pressed for beheading as a more merciful death.[12]

Finally, there was a lengthy dispute with certain extreme Lutherans such as Joachim Westphal over the nature of Christ's presence in the Lord's Supper. The Lutherans insisted that the body and blood of Christ were corporeally present in the Supper to be received by all who participated. This they founded on

---

11   Robert L. Reymond, *A New Systematic Theology of the Christian Faith* (New York: Nelson, 1998), 326–35.

12   Bruce Gordon, *Calvin* (New Haven: Yale University Press, 2009), 217–32.

the supposition that attributes of deity were communicated to Christ's humanity by virtue of the hypostatic union in the incarnation, so that the flesh and blood received the attribute of omnipresence.

Calvin was prepared to compromise if need be. In 1549 he reached agreement with Bullinger on the Lord's Supper in the wake of the Augsburg Interim of 1548 which parceled out Europe between Catholic and Lutheran jurisdictions, leaving the Reformed out in the cold. The need was to present a united front and not to insist on dotting every 'i' and crossing every 't.' The result was the *Consensus Tigurinus.*[13] Calvin also backed the 1541 agreement at Regensburg between Bucer and Melanchthon on the one side and Cardinals Contarini and Gropper of Rome over justification. Calvin was present at the Colloquy in a subordinate capacity. At that time there had never been an official pronouncement of any kind on justification. The two cardinals had come to accept justification by faith— and later suffered for this. Calvin saw that they had conceded much ground and gave his approval to the statement. Luther, on the other hand, disdained it. Calvin was also tolerant of other ecclesiastical polities. He congratulated Thomas Cranmer on the high honour God had given him by making him Archbishop of Canterbury, referring to it as a 'distinguished position,'[14] while he was reluctant to back Knox in his civil and ecclesiastical views.

Theology
In the nineteenth century it was commonplace to hold that Calvin's theology was dominated by predestination. From this perspective, Calvin and Calvinism were seen as one. Following

13   Philip Edgcumbe Hughes, *The Register of the Company of Pastors in Geneva at the Time of Calvin* (Grand Rapids: Eerdmans, 1966), 115–23.

14   Henry Beveridge, *Tracts and Letters, Part 2* (vol. 2 of *Selected Works of John Calvin;* 1849; repr., Grand Rapids: Baker, 1983), 347.

Karl Barth, these assumptions were revised. It was evident that in the definitive 1559 edition of the *Institute* election and predestination were not considered until the end of book 3, after everything else except the church. While it has been pointed out that Calvin considers providence and predestination to be inseparably linked, and that election undergirds all aspects of his view of salvation, it is also recognized that Calvin does not trace his whole theology logically from God's sovereign election.

Many attempts have been made to locate a central dogma in Calvin—a doctrine that governs the whole of his theology. Some have suggested union with Christ, the twofold knowledge of God, as in the *Institute*, the trinity—which is his doctrine of God, but all such attempts flounder with the realization that there is no one central unifying theme in Calvin. The reason for this is that Calvin attempts to follow Scripture wherever it may lead—and this directs him away from attempts to impose a logical straightjacket on the Bible. In fact, he can be very elusive if you try to pin him down on many different topics. He can even appear contradictory at times. This is due to his place as a seminal thinker like Augustine and it is perhaps why people have tried for centuries to work out what he was saying, different schools of interpretation forming in the process. It is not so with second rate thinkers—it is obvious what they are saying and few bother to discuss their work centuries later.

Calvin is certainly God-centred and trinitarian. It is a deeply conservative trinitarianism, strongly committed to the early councils, but is it influenced by the east or the west? It is clear that Augustine is the figure he cites most often and he is also committed to the western addition of the *filioque*. However, Calvin also read the Greek fathers as well, even though he did not cite them in context but more as weapons in debate.[15] Recent

---

15   Anthony N.S. Lane, *John Calvin: Student of the Church Fathers* (Grand Rapids: Baker, 1999), 3, 67–86.

studies have affirmed that Augustine was in full agreement with the trinitarian settlement reached in the east, so the question is largely irrelevant.[16]

As with Luther he did not take the position that the Bible is the only resource for theology. The phrase *sola scriptura* did not occur until the eighteenth century. The Bible was the highest court of appeal but not the only resource. Nor, like Luther, did he oppose tradition.

His quarrel was with the theologians of the Sorbonne—*les sophistes* as he often calls them.[17] Calvin opposed them by means of Scripture, the fathers (especially Augustine), and the best of the medievals. Aquinas had a big input, for Calvin and Aquinas are very close in more ways than not. It is noteworthy here that Aquinas was not *de rigeur* in Rome at the time—only in the nineteenth century was he accepted as a definitive teacher.

Contrary to Luther, he viewed the law as the rule of life for the Christian, and so had a far more positive estimate of the value of good works. He opposed the Lutherans' peculiar view of the ubiquity of Christ's human nature and Luther's insistence on consubstantiation in the eucharist. Justification by faith alone— which Calvin accepted and defended—was not central to the whole of theology, for our salvation is a part of the all-embracive plan of God for his creation. Thus for Calvin, the whole of life was to be lived under the jurisdiction of God. This leads us to his impact, for Calvin's theology was to have a huge effect not only on church but also culture.

16   Cf., Lewis Ayres, *Augustine and the Trinity* (Cambridge: Cambridge University Press, 2010).

17   Richard A. Muller, 'Scholasticism in Calvin: A Question of Relation and Disjunction,' in *Calvinus Sincerioris Religionis Vindex: Calvin as Protector of the Purer Religion* (Wilhelm H. Neuser; Kirksville, Missouri: Sixteenth Century Journal Publishers, 1997), 247–65.

HIS IMPACT

There is a timeless quality to Calvin's commentaries and his *Institutio*. He speaks to us today in a way that no commentator has before or since. His combination of theological exegesis and direct address to his congregation more often that not gets right to the heart of the matter in a way that often transcends time and place.

Many are those who have remarked that we can still see the impact of Calvin (certainly of Calvinism) in Geneva today, particularly if we compare it with other areas close by. Calvin's followers brought about reformation in Scotland, Holland, almost in France, in many parts of Germany, and exercised much influence in Poland, and Hungary. This they did against the odds, as a persecuted minority group, not with the patronage of a local prince or elector. In England, the Puritans gained control at one point but it has also been shown recently that the mainstream Anglican theology in late sixteenth century England actually was in agreement with the Reformed theology of the continental churches, of which Calvin was a prominent representative.[18] Richard Hooker as well as the Puritan William Perkins was a self-conscious Calvinist.[19] It was the nineteenth century Oxford movement, and John Henry Newman in particular, that successfully sold the myth that the Church of England adopted a *via media*, midway between Rome and Protestantism. This was not the case with Hooker at all nor with Cranmer before him.[20]

18   Cf. Diarmaid MacCulloch, *Thomas Cranmer: A Life* (New Haven: Yale University Press, 1996), 606–32; Bryan D. Spinks, *Two Faces of Elizabethan Anglican Theology: Sacraments and Salvation in the Thought of William Perkins and Richard Hooker* (Lanham, Maryland / London: Scarecrow Press, 1999).

19   Nigel Atkinson, *Richard Hooker and the Authority of Scripture, Tradition and Reason: Reformed Theologian of the Church of England?* (Carlisle, UK: Paternoster, 1997); W. Torrance Kirby, *Richard Hooker's Doctrine of the Royal Supremacy* (Leiden: E.J. Brill, 1990).

20   MacCulloch, *Cranmer*, 606–32.

Revolution followed Calvin's views—in Scotland, Holland, England in the seventeenth century leading to the Glorious Revolution of 1688. In 1776 one of the signatories of the Declaration of Independence was The Rev. John Witherspoon, a Calvinist from Scotland who had himself read and studied the great man. We are probably familiar with the theory of Max Weber, now largely undermined, that Calvinism was the engine powering the dynamic growth of capitalism.[21] However, it is clearly difficult to understand the modern world apart from reference to Calvin.

FOR FURTHER READING

With Calvin there is such a vast range of primary and secondary sources that it is a huge question as to where to begin.

Primary sources
Calvin, John. *Institutes of the Christian Religion.* Edited by Ford Lewis Battles. John T. McNeill. Philadelphia: Westminster Press, 1960.
Calvin: *Theological Treatises.* J.K.S. Reid. Philadelphia: Westminster Press, 1954.
Hughes, Philip Edgcumbe. *The Register of the Company of Pastors in Geneva at the Time of Calvin.* Grand Rapids: Eerdmans, 1966.

Secondary sources
Gordon, Bruce. *Calvin.* New Haven: Yale University Press, 2009.
Lane, Anthony N.S. *John Calvin: Student of the Church Fathers.* Grand Rapids: Baker, 1999.

21   Max Weber, *The Protestant Ethic and the Spirit of Capitalism* (New York: Charles Scribner's Sons, 1958).

McKee, Elsie Anne. 'Exegesis, Theology, and Development in Calvin's Institutio: A Methodological Suggestion.' Pages 154–72 in *Probing the Reformed Tradition*. Elsie Anne McKee, ed. Louisville, Kentucky: Westminster John Knox Press, 1989.

———. *John Calvin on the Diaconate and Liturgical Almsgiving*. Geneva: Librairie Droz, 1984.

Olson, Jeannine. *Calvin and Social Welfare: Deacons and the Bourse Francaise*. Selinsgrove, Pennsylvania: Susquehanna University Press, 1989.

Parker, T.H.L. *Calvin's Preaching*. Louisville, Kentucky: Westminster John Knox Press, 1992.

10

JOHN WESLEY (1703–1791)

LIFE AND WORK

Background and education

John Wesley was born on 17 June 1703, the son of the rector of the parish of Epworth in Lincolnshire, Samuel Wesley (not to be confused with the nineteenth century cathedral organist, composer and hymn writer of the same name, who was his great-grandson and the grandson of Charles Wesley) and his wife Susanna. Epworth is a small village in a drab, flat, remote area. Samuel persisted as rector from 1693 until his death in 1734, despite the hatred of his parishioners—probably justified due to his obstinate pig-headedness. On occasions the locals burnt Wesley's crops, maimed his animals and most likely launched an arson attack that burnt the rectory to the ground when John Wesley was only six. The father deserted his wife for a time before John was conceived, because she would not say 'Amen' to the prayer for King William III.[1] It was John Wesley's mother, Susanna, who had the greatest influence on him. The family was home-schooled in their early years, as was the custom. The family theology was high-church Anglicanism, with Puritan discipline (Susanna's father Samuel Annesley was a well-known Puritan minister). At the age of 10, Wesley was sent to Charterhouse, then and now one of the leading public schools (private schools in American terms). From there he entered Christ Church, Oxford (part of Oxford University). He received a BA degree in 1724, became a Fellow of Lincoln College (part of Oxford University) and was ordained a priest in the Church of England.

The fellowship at Lincoln College provided Wesley with a comfortable income that would lapse if he married. No teaching duties, or even residence, was required apart from a certain service on a roster basis, unless the Master of Lincoln requested it. However, from 1729 Wesley lived in Oxford, served as a tutor and preached regularly at the University and elsewhere. This was a life he found very congenial.

At this time Wesley was strongly influenced by the tradition of disciplined, legalistic piety of Thomas à Kempis, Jeremy Taylor and William Law. In this line of thought Christ is mainly an example to be imitated by rigorous self-examination, and the keeping of a spiritual journal. We will ask the question later of how far Wesley underwent a change later on, for it is very evident that—for all his denials—this strain of legalistic pietism never left him. When Wesley was a Fellow, his brother Charles—six years younger—had come to the University. Together with a growing group of like-minded ardent spiritual devotees, from both town and gown, including among their number the young George Whitefield, they formed what became known as the Holy Club.

---

1   On Samuel Wesley's character, see V.H.H. Green, *John Wesley* (London: Nelson, 1964), 49f; Henry D. Rack, *Reasonable Enthusiast: John Wesley and the Rise of Methodism* (London: Epworth Press, 1989), 48–50.

This was not merely a gathering for narcissistic introspection but it engaged widely and vigorously in social action, especially prison visitation and the education of orphans. Wesley was the dominant force. His rigorous, organized approach to everything imaginable brought upon him and his followers the catchphrase 'Methodists.'

Missionary in Georgia

In 1735 Wesley accepted an offer from the Society for the Propagation of Christian Knowledge (SPCK) to go to Georgia (the colony) as a missionary. Georgia had recently been founded by James Oglethorpe, a friend of the family. Wesley sailed to become vicar of Savannah. On the way over he was greatly impressed by a group of German Moravians, followers of Count von Zinzendorf, who remained calm and full of faith when the boat seemed likely to be sunk in a raging north Atlantic storm in the middle of January. Both in Georgia and later, on his return to England, he was to have continued contact with the Moravians, although he grew to recognize their unbiblical quietism as a threat to the gospel.

His experience in Georgia had some success, insofar as the Savannah congregation grew and a number of small group meetings had formed there and elsewhere under his direction— the shape of things to come. However, it ended in near disaster. He fell in love with Sophie Hopkey, the niece of the chief magistrate. On several occasions he effectively proposed marriage, only almost immediately to profess his determination to remain single. After a while, Sophie—disgusted—suddenly married someone else, of meagre means and abilities. Wesley then imposed church discipline on her in retaliation. The magistrate brought charges against Wesley and issued an order forbidding him to leave the colony. He was indicted by a grand jury. But before anything could be done he escaped, with his colleagues and boarded a ship back to England. The official

records state that he 'ran away.'[2] Back in England, the trustees
of SPCK, according to Lord Egmont—one of their number—
recorded that he appeared to them 'a very odd mixture of a man,
an enthusiast, and at the same time a hypocrite, distasteful to the
greater part of the inhabitants and an incendiary of the people
against the magistracy.'[3]

Aldersgate Street 24 May 1738
In Oxford, to which he returned, and also in London, Wesley
continued his contacts with the Moravians and resumed his
ascetic disciplines at the Holy Club. The Moravians had spurred
him to seek assurance of his salvation. One of their leaders in
Georgia, Spangenberg, had asked him whether the Spirit of God
bore witness with his spirit that he was a child of God, whether
he knew Jesus Christ, and whether Christ had saved him? Wesley
commented 'What have I learned of myself in the meantime?
Why, what I the least of all suspected, that I, who went to
America to convert others, was never myself converted to God.'[4]

On 21 May 1738, Pentecost, Charles Wesley received assurance
of his salvation. Three days later, Wesley attended choral evensong
in St Paul's Cathedral, London. The choir sang William Purcell's
anthem, 'Out of the deep have I called unto thee, O Lord', from
Psalm 130. Immediately Wesley opened his Bible and the first
thing he read was the sentence 'Thou art not far from the kingdom
of God.' Random scanning of isolated biblical sentences was, and
ever continued to be, both Wesleys' basis for decision making.
He went at once to a society meeting at Aldersgate Street, where
someone—we know not who—read from Luther's preface to his
Lectures on Romans. Wesley famously records 'About a quarter

---

2   V.H.H. Green, *The Young Mr. Wesley* (London: Epworth Press, 1961), 265;
Rack, *Reasonable Enthusiast*, 124–30, 258; Iain H. Murray, *Wesley and Men Who
Followed* (Edinburgh: Banner of Truth, 2003), 8.
3   Green, *Wesley*, 53.
4   Green, *Wesley*, 52.

to nine, while he was describing the change which God works in the heart through faith in Christ, I felt my heart strangely warmed. I felt I did trust in Christ, Christ alone for salvation; and an assurance was given me that He had taken away my sins, even mine, and saved me from the law of sin and death.' Wesley's reference to the time is typical, for he recorded meticulously every minute of every day.

Scholars continue to debate exactly what happened in his Aldersgate Street experience. Was it a conversion from unbelief to faith? Or was it a sudden reception of assurance? The matter is clouded because Wesley's theology forbad him having a proper doctrine of assurance of salvation! This was due to his opposition to the doctrine of the perseverance of the saints. As a consequence, while for Wesley it was possible to have assurance of God's favour in the present, there is no possibility of assurance of his favour for eternity since there is a chance one may fall from grace. Was it a new understanding, in a vivid and personal way, of the gospel that stopped short of a conversion, since he had always believed these things? One clue is that throughout his later career Wesley dates the time he began to believe and preach salvation through Christ alone and justification by faith to 1738. Again, in his standard sermons he speaks of the 'almost Christian' in contrast to the 'altogether Christian,' which might be paraphrased in today's popular evangelical jargon as the difference between a nominal Christian and a born-again Christian.[5] On balance we must defer to his own assessment of where he stood before and after this event. As with the Moravians, he now claimed that on this date he was justified by faith alone, while before he had been trusting in his own righteousness.

---

5 'The Almost Christian: Preached at St Mary's Oxford, before the University on July 25, 1741, in *The Works of The Rev. John Wesley* (London: Wesleyan-Methodist Book-Room, 1872), 5:17–25.

Itinerant ministry erupts

A sudden new development occurred within the year, one that was to change the entire direction of Wesley's life. His friend George Whitefield began preaching in the Bristol area, outside the bounds of the parochial system and outside church buildings, a radical departure from proper ecclesiastical practice. Of importance was that a large proportion of the population were entirely unchurched and, for social reasons, were unlikely ever to darken the doors of a parish church. At Bristol, Whitefield preached to hard-bitten coal miners. As he preached that Jesus came to call not the righteous but sinners, he saw on their coal-blackened faces, 'white gutters made by their tears, which plentifully ran down their black cheeks, as they came out of their coal pits.'[6] Whitefield, not one to organize, called Wesley in for help so that he could move on to newer pastures.[7]

From then until his death Wesley itinerated and preached incessantly. In all he preached 40,000 times in 53 years. We know this because of his meticulous and comprehensive journals in which he accounted for every moment of every day—one of the most tedious and impersonal documents in history according to many scholars. This amounts to an average of twice per day every day for fifty three years! To do so he travelled around 250,000 miles—an average of 13 miles per day every day for fifty three years until the age of 88. This was travel by foot or horseback, along poor, muddy, rutted roads for the most part in the days before tarmac. It entailed staying at squalid inns, with rough uncomfortable beds, eating poor, unappetising food. Wesley read, wrote, and prayed on horseback in full view of his entourage. He had no time or place for privacy. He travelled the length and breadth of the country, and Ireland too. His main circuit was London-Bristol-Newcastle, the equivalent of a large triangle. In

6   Green, *Wesley*, 73.
7   Green, *Wesley*, 73–74.

the course of this he would divert to towns and villages along the way. He would gather a group of converts, form them into societies, and later visit them to exercise discipline. In Wesley's own words, he believed himself to be called to preach 'to the vulgar herd, the poor, base, stupid part of mankind.'[8]

The societies

Wesley founded a movement, whereas Whitefield did not do so. This was in large part due to Wesley's organizing genius and enormous attention to detail. He grouped his converts into societies. He provided General Rules for these societies, to which members were required to adhere. Members had to do all the good they could, avoid evil (the main kinds were meticulously listed), and attend the means of grace. There were quarterly examinations of the members, and class tickets were awarded to all who passed. This kept the growth of the movement slow in the eighteenth century, there being only 72,000 members at the time of Wesley's death.

Strong lay leadership was evident throughout the movement, at all levels. Lay preachers, mainly uneducated, were required to preach nothing that was not in Wesley's published sermons. Thus, the lay leadership was strictly under Wesley's control. Wesley published over 400 books and pamphlets for his people. His published sermons ran to 8 volumes, his collected works to 32 volumes. In addition, he produced textbooks in a variety of subjects, reminding us that he was a Fellow of Lincoln College, Oxford. He also founded a school at Kingswood, in Bristol, and in his later career supported the early work of William Wilberforce, eventually successful in ending the slave trade.

Wesley's preaching was hardly remarkable. In this, Whitefield was by far his superior, despite his own lack of significant content. Indeed, Wesley was compared by one observer to a

8   *The Works of John Wesley* (1872; repr., Grand Rapids: Baker, 1979), 1:667.

marble statue, with one exception—Wesley moved his hands on occasions to turn the pages of his manuscript.

Wesley and the Church of England

To their deaths, the Wesleys remained staunch clergymen of the Church of England. Wesley urged his followers to attend their local parish church. Society meetings were timed deliberately so as not to conflict with the services of the parish church. He considered it his task 'to reform the nation, especially the Church [of England].' While many Anglican clergy opposed Wesley, some on grounds of ecclesiastical decorum, others due to the excesses that attended some meetings, others on doctrinal grounds because of his Arminianism, nonetheless he received a welcome from many others, some of whom opened their churches to his ministry.

However, it was inevitable that the new societies would eventually become autonomous. This happened soon after his death in 1791. In fact, Wesley himself unwittingly assisted in the process by sanctioning the ordination of ministers in the societies that emerged in the American colonies. These ordinations, out of necessity, were conducted by a clergyman who was not a bishop. Wesley referred to him as a superintendent. This was a direct flouting of settled Anglican procedure. Moreover, from 1744 he established a series of preachers' conferences to secure uniformity of doctrine and disciplined Christian living. These conferences had published minutes which became effectively a handbook for the societies. It is notable that doctrine was reached collectively.

Lack of judgment and marital collapse

Wesley had a marked lack of understanding of human nature. This was seen in the Sophie Hopkey saga in Georgia but it also came to expression in the almost surreal soap opera events surrounding Grace Murray. Grace Murray was a young widow, a follower of Wesley. She fell under his spell and, with his full encouragement, accompanied him on preaching tours, including one to Ireland. One of Wesley's preachers, John Bennet, was also pursuing her. In an uncanny rerun of the Georgia debacle, Wesley offered her marriage. 'I am convinced God has called you to be my fellow labourer in the gospel…now we must part for a time, but if we meet again I trust we shall part no more,' he had told her. But then he decided that they should not part at all, and took her with him on the next phase of his itinerations. However, he reversed that decision in order to preach in Derbyshire, recording 'I left her in Cheshire with John Bennet [!] and went on my way rejoicing'!! Eventually, Grace was distraught at the tension and uncertainty Wesley generated. Charles Wesley learned of the possible marriage with consternation, since Grace was socially his brother's inferior. He rode across half the country on horseback in hot pursuit and whisked Grace away from his brother's entourage while he was away preaching, on the pretext of a letter purporting to be from John renouncing her, a letter he had written himself! She left post haste with Charles, who took her to Bennet and had them married. John, finding Grace gone, remained passive until summoned to Leeds by an urgent letter from Whitefield. Whitefield, on his arrival, informed Wesley of the wedding. Soon Charles appeared! John refused to speak to him. Charles shouted at his brother that he was a heathen or a publican. Whitefield bawled his eyes out. They prayed, they cried—then into the hysterical gathering came…John Bennet! He and Wesley did not speak but kissed and wept.[9]

If Wesley's conduct in this sorry tale was vacillating, naive and inept (Bennet later became a Calvinist minister), worse was to follow. In 1751 he did marry. His wife, Molly Vazeille, was the widow of a prosperous London banker, with four grown children. Charles was enraged as before, this time justifiably so. Wesley should have seen that his work precluded marriage to any but

9   Green, *The Young Mr. Wesley*, 202; Rack, *Reasonable Enthusiast*, 258–64.

a devoted follower of his who might be prepared to endure the same privations and unsettled lifestyle as he did. A comfortably off middle-aged London widow with a grown family did not come into this category. Moreover, she was a jealous and bitter woman. Part of her bitterness must have been occasioned by Wesley's interminable absences. Additionally, Wesley had a free and easy manner with young female followers. Nothing improper ever occurred—his life was so public this was impossible—but he devoted excessive attention to them and wrote in unguarded terms. He wrote to a Mrs. Sarah Ryan, a young woman he appointed as housekeeper at Kingswood School, Bristol 'I cannot think of you without thinking of God.'[10] In fact, Sarah (aged 33) was at the time a trigamist! Molly wrote to Wesley, 'the whore now serving you has three husbands living.'[11]

By 1758 Wesley's wife left him—permanently. Thereafter contact between them was increasingly acrimonious. She rifled his correspondence for reasons to defame him. In his last letter to her he wrote 'if you were to live a thousand years, you could not undo the mischief that you have done. And till you have done all you can towards it, I bid you farewell.'[12] When Molly died, Wesley did not attend her funeral.[13] At the very least it is clear that Wesley had an almost stupefying lack of understanding of human beings, of how they think and feel. This is borne out by his journals, which for all their vast and comprehensive coverage, are devoid of human interest, and by Wesley's entire life, which for half a century completely lacked any semblance of privacy.

---

10   John Telford, *The Letters of John Wesley, A.M.* (London: Epworth Press, 1931), 4:3.

11   Rack, *Reasonable Enthusiast*, 268; L. Tyerman, *The Life and Times of The Rev. John Wesley, M.A.: Founder of the Methodists. Fourth Edition.* (London: Hodder and Stoughton, 1878), 2:285f.

12   Rack, *Reasonable Enthusiast*, 266.

13   For discussions of Wesley's marriage, see Rack, *Reasonable Enthusiast*, 264–69; Murray, *Wesley*, 45–46.

Perhaps this was simply the flip side of a highly singular life. No one could have travelled all he did, or preached as much, without some compensating deficiencies. The obituary notice in the Gentlemans' Magazine described him as 'one of the most extraordinary characters this or any age ever produced.'[14]

Controversy

Wesley was militantly opposed to Calvinism. In 1740 he published a sermon 'Free grace' denouncing Calvinism in scathing terms. It represents God as worse than the devil, he claimed. He dismissed John Cennick as Master of Kingswood School because he had embraced Calvinist views. He persuaded his preachers to publish anti-Calvinist minutes of their 1770 conference.

He had prearranged with his friend, George Whitefield, that one of them would preach at the funeral of whoever died first. When Whitefield died prematurely in America in 1770, Wesley preached to an immense crowd, referring to two basic doctrines of Whitefield—the new birth and justification by faith—but making no mention of predestination. This raised an outcry among many evangelicals who had, to a point, backed him. These included the influential Countess of Huntingdon. Then the redoubtable Augustus Toplady, composer of 'Rock of ages' and 'A debtor to mercy alone,' pitched in with a pamphlet attacking Arminianism. Wesley republished it, with annotations ridiculing and purporting that the refutation was from Toplady himself! This scurrilous tactic raised a furore. Rowland Hill, a leading Calvinist minister of the day, stated that Wesley 'has been a proverb for his contradictions for about thirty years.' Toplady himself commented acidly, 'Time, sire, has already whitened your locks; and the hour must shortly come, which will transmit you to the tribunal of that God, on whose sovereignty

14   Cited in R.P. Heitzenrater, 'Wesley, J.' in Timothy Larson, *Biographical Dictionary of Evangelicals* (Leicester: Inter-Varsity Press, 2003), 715.

a great part of your life has been one continued assault.'[15] In 1773 he added, 'I believe him to be the most rancorous hater of the gospel system that ever appeared in England,' and accused him—unfairly—of Pelagianism,[16] of being 'a spitting journalizer,'[17] of 'shameless plagiarism,'[18] and of having written a 'wretched bundle of plagiarisms on the New Testament.'[19] As if to add icing to the cake, Toplady fumed, 'May your name, sir, after all that you have done, be found at last in that Book of Life against which you have so daringly exclaimed! May your person be interested in that only perfect righteousness, on which you have so unhappily trampled!'[20]

THEOLOGY

Wesley regarded his theology as embodied in a series of Standard Sermons. There were 44 of them, although in the United States it is considered that there are 53. He maintained that he was following the teaching of The Thirty-Nine Articles of Religion of the Church of England. This is recognized as a Reformed confession. However, he introduced some clear deviations from the Articles, notably in his doctrine of sanctification and in his abandonment of their clear, robust predestinarianism.

He correctly opposed the quietism of the Moravians, who had been so influential at the time of his conversion. They insisted that when under conviction of sin, one must stop all action—stop doing good works, stop receiving the sacraments, stop attending church and the preaching of the word of God. Instead,

15 *The Works of Augustus Toplady, B.A., Late Vicar of Broad Hembury, Devon* (Harrisonburg, Virginia: Sprinkle Publications, 1987), 761.

16 *Works*, 52–54.

17 *Works*, 227.

18 *Works*, 754, 756.

19 *Works*, 205 note.

20 *Works*, 761.

one must wait for the Lord, resting in quietness. Wesley rejected this as serious error. He stressed that we need good works as well as faith, that the faith through which we are justified is never alone but always accompanied by its fruit.

However, as we have seen, he also opposed the Reformed faith, being a staunch Arminian. He had a particular antipathy to the doctrines of election and predestination. In preaching George Whitefield's funeral sermon, he omitted all reference to Whitefield's Calvinism. His militant anti-Calvinism provoked a split among his followers. The Calvinistic Methodists broke away. Eventually located mainly in Wales, they became effectively Presbyterian.

Wesley believed in the total depravity of man. In his natural state man is blind to the things of God. However, this is to an extent mitigated by prevenient grace (*prevenio*, to go before)—universal, efficacious grace, giving sinners a natural ability to respond to the gospel. This grace is irresistible. Here Wesley agrees with Calvinism that there is irresistible grace. However, whereas the Reformed maintain that this brings about saving faith in the elect and is thus particular, not universal, Wesley considered it universal but non-saving. It enables fallen man to accept—or appropriate—the gospel, if he wills to do so. It restores a measure of free will and enlightens the mind so that the natural man can see dimly certain attributes of God. It is sufficient to enable people to respond to the gospel by their free will.

A lynchpin of Wesley's strategy was to attack nominal Christianity. One of the Standard Sermons, 'The almost Christian,' preached at Oxford in July 1741, was aimed at ministers and other professing Christians. The 'almost Christian' is an honest person, sincere in his religious belief and practice. He obeys the law, abstains from theft and slander. He seeks to order his life in a way pleasing to God. He attends the means of grace and participates in, or leads, family worship. However, Wesley contrasts this with 'the altogether Christian.' This person is marked by the love of God and neighbour. The 'altogether Christian' has a faith that brings forth repentance. This was a hallmark of Wesley's preaching and theology—which is why this sermon is one of the Standard Sermons. It demonstrates a critical attitude to Christian nurture and paves the way for his stress on a crisis experience that he terms the new birth.[21]

Justification by faith was also central. For Wesley, justification was simply pardon, forgiveness of sins. He carefully distinguished it from sanctification. Scholars debate whether Wesley accepted that the righteousness of Christ is imputed to believers. The evidence of the sermons is that he did,[22] but he was somewhat equivocal since he feared antinomianism and often coupled references to the imputation of Christ's righteousness with reference to the implantation of Christ's righteousness in believers (sanctification as Reformed theology understands it).[23] Here the continued influence of William Law is evident.[24] Did Wesley really change? Can he be accused of legalism, of neo-nomianism?

Moreover, due to his doctrine of prevenient grace, those who are justified by faith are in some way responsible for the fact that they are justified.[25] This is a highly significant departure from Calvin and the Reformed tradition. These people have co-operated with God—synergism—and so once again the graciousness of justification is called into question.

Wesley stressed the necessity of the new birth. In this, a person feels the mighty working of the Holy Spirit in his heart. It happens quickly, and is followed by the process of sanctification.

21   *Works*, 5:17–25.
22   *Works*, 5:241–42.
23   See the discussion in Murray, *Wesley*, 224–27.
24   Wesley refers frequently to Law; see *Works*, 14:445.
25   Toplady argued that Wesley made faith the cause of justification, and our obedience of Christ the cause of eternal life. In this case we must be aware that Toplady was no disinterested witness; see *Works*, 761.

He was highly critical of those who said they were always a Christian. The new birth is marked by faith (confidence in the mercy of God, victory over the power of sin—actual, outward sin), hope and love. This is in contrast to the general experience of many raised in Christian homes, who can never identify such an experience. Timothy was one of them (2 Tim. 1:5). So were the children of the church addressed by the apostle Paul and instructed as to their Christian privileges and responsibilities in the Lord (Eph. 6:1–3).

One of the most controversial and far-reaching of Wesley's teachings was that of entire sanctification, or Christian perfection. He never held that it was possible to be sinlessly perfect in this life but he did strongly teach—and it was one of his three or four most common emphases—that the Christian could arrive at a state where he wholly loved God and was free from actual and known sin. This is connected with his view of justification already mentioned.

We have already remarked on his lifelong opposition to predestination. He regarded those who taught it to hold that God was worse than the devil. Due to his opposition to predestination—and his denial of the perseverance of the saints—he could have no doctrine of assurance of final salvation, only assurance of present salvation. The reason for this is that he held it to be possible for a true believer to fall from grace.

Did Wesley preach the gospel? Was he a legalist? His main concern was definitely the danger of antinomianism. This explains the vehemence of his hatred for the Reformed faith. He never really abandoned the teaching of Thomas à Kempis and William Law. His Aldersgate Street experience left that unchanged. If anything it strengthened it. This is seen by his methods with the societies. Continuance in the societies was contingent on abstaining from known sins, which he defined himself, on taking no alcoholic beverages of any kind, and the practice of approved good works. Members had to be willing to undergo rigorous exposure of their faults by others in open sessions, to confess publicly all known sin and all temptations they had faced. Women were to wear no needless ornaments.[26] This was a thorough going system of control, with Wesley himself exerting total domination of all Methodist preachers and society leaders. On visiting the societies, Wesley would frequently expel large numbers who had not measured up to his demands.

Charles Wesley's hymns were intended specifically to spread his brother's theology. They all refer to universal salvation and the possibility of Christian perfection. We must never forget that Charles Wesley composed these hymns as a deliberate and self-conscious assault on the Reformed faith, as a means of inculcating unbiblical teachings.[27] Charles Wesley's hymns for the most part cannot be sung without modification or reserve. This is so even though many of them, without these elements, are among the best ever written.

IMPACT

It has been claimed that Wesley saved England from a violent revolution like in France. This is probably not the case, since the context socially and politically in the two countries was so different. But there is little doubt that he left a profound and lasting impact on wide swathes of society. The most tangible long-term impact was, of course, the formation of the Methodist Church. Here Wesley contrasts with Whitefield, who left no such legacy. Even so, this was against Wesley's own intentions, for he hoped to renew and revive the Church of England and remained an ordained Anglican clergyman until he died.

Beyond that, the holiness movement (including the Keswick movement), with its offspring in Pentecostalism and the

---

26   *Works*, 8:269–74.
27   See J.R. Tyson, 'Wesley, Charles,' in Larson, *BDE*, 711.

charismatic movement, owes its genesis and many of its emphases to Wesley. The stress on special experiences of the Holy Spirit,
on sanctification as a post-conversion experience, a critical attitude to Christian nurture, all trace theological lineage back to
Wesley and the evangelical movement of the eighteenth century.
Today's evangelicalism in north America is dominated by his
legacy.

There was a deep social impact too. Wesley reached a different
strata of society than the Church of England was doing. Schools,
medical clinics, housing, pension funds, diaconal ventures,
all stemmed from Methodist action. Wesley in his later years
attacked the slave trade and supported the young William
Wilberforce. Beyond that there was a strong influence on the
emergence and development of the Trade Union movement and,
eventually, the Labour Party. A favourite question on history and
politics examination papers in England at one time was 'The
Labour Party owes more to Methodism than to Marx. Discuss.'

However, Wesley brought about a move away from historic
Christianity. The focus of the great tradition of the church had
been the trinity, the person and work of Christ, the church
and sacraments. Now it shifted to the individual and personal
salvation, to introspection and legalistic control.[28]

Wesley's views led to a disparagement of God's covenant
and its promises. His emphasis on spiritual experience has led
to a glorification of emotionalism. He had an unbiblical and
misguided view of sanctification, that has plagued the church
ever since. He passed on all the errors of Arminianism. The
effect of his movement, despite his own best wishes, has been
the downplaying of the church and sacraments. As such, it was
an adaptation of conservative Christianity to the world of the
Enlightenment. As Toplady alleged, the most part of his life was

---

28   Robert Letham, 'Is Evangelicalism Christian?' *EQ* 67, no. 1 (1995): 3–33.

a systematic, full blooded assault on the sovereignty of God. His legacy is at best mixed and is with us still.

FOR FURTHER READING

Collins, K.J. *Wesley on Salvation: A Study in the Standard Sermons.* Grand Rapids: Zondervan, 1989.

Green, V.H.H. *John Wesley.* London: Nelson, 1964.

Oden, T.C. *John Wesley's Scriptural Christianity: A Plain Exposition of his Teaching on Christian Doctrine.* Grand Rapids: Zondervan, 1994.

Outler, A.C., ed. *John Wesley.* New York: Oxford University Press, 1964.

Rack, H.D. *Reasonable Enthusiast.* Philadelphia: Trinity Press International, 1989.

Tyerman, L. *The Life and Times of the Rev. John Wesley.* London: Hodder and Stoughton, 1871.

11

J.W. NEVIN (1803–86)
AND THE MERCERSBURG THEOLOGY[1]

LIFE AND MINISTRY

John Williamson Nevin was raised a Presbyterian in rural central Pennsylvania. He attended Union College, New York, receiving a BA in 1821, at the age of eighteen. While there he came into contact with the new school Presbyterianism that had been influenced by the revival movement. After a spell on his father's farm, he attended Princeton Theological Seminary, graduating in 1826. He studied under Archibald Alexander and Charles Hodge. When Hodge took an extended period of leave to study in Germany Nevin took his place from 1826–28. From

---

1   Much of this paper has emerged from notes of an unpublished lecture I gave in 1996. Biographical material came from a variety of sources and is generally known information.

1828–40 he was on the faculty of Western Theological Seminary, Pittsburgh, a newly started Presbyterian seminary.

In 1840 he was called to the German Reformed seminary at Mercersburg, Pennsylvania. The German Reformed Church was rural and isolated, largely located in Lancaster County, Pennsylvania. Mercersburg was, and is, a small village in the mountains west of Harrisburg, the State capital. Nevin may not even have heard of it before the invitation. By this time, Nevin had become convinced of the degree to which new school piety, with its emphasis on conversionism and personal individual piety, could lead to subjectivism.

Nevin was increasingly influenced by the philosophical movement of romanticism. When his colleague Frederick A. Rauch died, Nevin edited the second edition of his exposition of the philosophy of Hegel, the first in America. Rauch stressed the priority of ideals behind actuals (observable phenomena). The German church historian, Johann Neander, aroused in Nevin an esteem for the Fathers, and also pointed him to a theory of organic development in church history[2] which reinforced his exposure to Hegel. Neander also stressed the centrality of the resurrection of Christ for world history, the supernatural being a real presence in the physical world. Together, these influences drew Nevin towards an appreciation of the importance of the incarnation, and of the church as a spiritual entity, the central means by which God ministered salvation in the world through Christ.[3]

This was a world apart from American evangelical Protestantism as it had developed, with its powerfully individualistic slant, focusing on conversion and individual spiritual experience,

---

2   Ideas of organic growth and development were rife at the time. John Henry Newman produced his theory of the development of doctrine in his *An Essay on the Development of Christian Doctrine* in 1845 and shortly afterwards Charles Darwin applied these ideas to biology in *The Origin of Species* in 1859.

3   D. Hart, *John Williamson Nevin: High-Church Calvinist* (Phillipsburg, New Jersey: Presbyterian & Reformed, 2005) 73–7.

on the emotional manipulation of the anxious bench, while speaking nothing of the sacraments or of the church.

At Mercersburg, Nevin came into conflict with revivalist techniques that were threatening to infiltrate his own congregation. A preacher, William Ramsay, an old classmate of Nevin's from Princeton, candidating for the vacant pulpit with the overwhelming support of the congregation, at the end of a service asked those under conviction of their guilt and unworthiness to come forward to the 'anxious bench' to receive prayer. This was a method introduced by the Arminian—almost Pelagian—evangelist Charles Finney. At the close Nevin, asked to speak a few words, remarked that creeping 'about from one corner of the church to the other until their knees were sore and bleeding' was of no avail. Ramsay was called, Nevin wrote to him expressing misgivings about his methods, and Ramsay declined the call.[4]

Nevin was joined on the faculty in 1843 by the young Philip Schaff from German Lutheranism. The next decade saw an amazing outburst of creative energy amid great controversy, which we will consider below. Nevin continued at Mercersburg until 1853, resigning from the seminary faculty in 1851, and serving as President of Marshall College, the German Reformed college, from 1841–53.

At the time of his resignation, Nevin had suffered a breakdown and so he retired in 1853. From 1861 he returned to Marshall College and was President again from 1866 to 1876. Schaff's main work came later, particularly after his move to Union Theological Seminary, New York, when he produced monumental works such as his Creeds of Christendom, History of the Church, Nicene and Post-Nicene Fathers, Schaff-Herzog Encyclopedia, and founded the American Society for Church History, together with his extensive ecumenical activities.

4   Ibid., 90.

Principal themes

What has made Nevin retrospectively regarded by many as one of the most important American theologians, when he was ignored or vilified in his own day and is virtually unknown elsewhere?

Nevin was virtually alone in opposing the rampant individualism and anti-ecclesial direction of American Protestantism. He and Schaff were almost the only ones in America in touch with German theology, which had led the way since the eighteenth century. Theirs was an attempt to interact with the high church movements in German Lutheranism and Anglo-Catholicism.

For Nevin there were two distinct but related problems in American Christianity. There was the revivalist movement spearheaded by Charles Finney that pressed for individual decisions, using powerfully manipulative means, was largely critical of or disconnected from the church and, above all, held to a Pelagian view of salvation. Secondly, there was what Nevin called, clumsily, 'Puritanism.' By this he meant the anthropocentric, individualist piety that developed in the eighteenth century revivals and had taken hold of American Protestantism. Even Hodge and Princeton was part of this thinking. It helped the rapid proliferation of sects, each claiming the authority of the Bible for their distinctive doctrines and also downgrading the sacraments, church and ministry. In opposition, Nevin called for a return to Christian nurture within the church, based on the Word and sacraments, catechetical instruction, and pastoral visitation. He maintained the church was divinely ordained as a living organism bearing the life that brought salvation. In this Nevin represented a call to return to the churchly nature of the Christian faith in the midst of rampant individualism.

MAJOR WORKS

The Anxious Bench (1843)

In this, his first major work, Nevin launched an assault on the revivalist techniques, the Pelagian doctrine of self-salvation held by Finney, the individualism on which the techniques were based, and the sectarianism they spawned. Instead, he advocated a system of church-based Christian nurture, oriented around the Word and sacraments. Baptism, and a regular process of catechizing in the home, pastoral visitation, and attendance on the ministry of the Word and the Lord's Supper were the means God has appointed for the growth and advancement of his church. Salvation comes to sinners through the institutions and agencies of the church 'which God has appointed, and clothed with power expressly for this end.' So 'where the system of the catechism prevails, great account is made of the church' for Christ lives in the church, and through the church in its particular members.'[5] This is so since 'the extraordinary is found ever to stand in the ordinary.'[6]

The Sect System (1848)

At the time Nevin wrote, there were eighty-five new denominations or sects in the USA.[7] Nevin deplored this development. Each of these sects claimed the supreme authority of the Bible for their existence, together with the right of private interpretation, and many also stressed justification by the imputed righteousness of

---

5   John Williamson Nevin, *The Anxious Bench* (2nd ed.; Chambersburg, Pa.: Publication Office of the German Reformed Church, 1844), reprinted in *Catholic and Reformed: Selected Theological Writings of John Williamson Nevin* (ed. Charles Yrigoyen and George H. Bricker; Pittsburgh Original Texts and Translation Series 3; Pittsburgh: Pickwick, 1978), 110–11.

6   Ibid., 118–9.

7   There are now countless thousands, many more if independent churches are taken into consideration.

Christ. Common to all, in Nevin's estimation, was a Baptistic theology, since this was connected directly to their individualist premises. As a consequence, they devalued or ignored the historic creeds, since the sects' reason for being was the claim that they and they alone had a right understanding of the Bible and so possessed a direct line to God. Thus the church's past, its teaching and tradition, was irrelevant. This fitted closely with the American penchant for the present at the expense of the past. Since the country was new and had self-consciously rejected tradition, the proliferation of sects was a natural development. Following this, the sects despised or rejected an ordained ministry and had a low view of the sacraments, invariably rejecting infant baptism and having at best a Zwinglian theory of the Lord's Supper. Nevin argued their stress on the private interpretation of the Bible was the cause of their constant proliferation. Instead, he claimed, God had given the church as a life-bearing revelation, and as the context out of whose life the Bible was to be interpreted.

The Mystical Presence (1846)[8]
This was Nevin's *magnum opus*, in which he unfolded his sacramental theology, and with it a devastating critique of the Reformed churches of his day. In this book he went beyond a criticism of revivalists like Finney or the sects spawned from individualism. This pressed closer to home, in the sense that it was a challenge to the Reformed churches from which he had come.

Nevin's basic assumptions:
Foundational to all he said in the book is the assumption of the primacy of the life of the church, which flows to the Christian ultimately from Christ. He states, 'The life of the single Christian

---

8   John W. Nevin, *The Mystical Presence: A Vindication of the Reformed or Calvinistic Doctrine of the Holy Eucharist* (Philadelphia: J.P. Lippincott & Co., 1846).

can be real and healthful only as it is born from the general life
of the church…We are Christians…by partaking in the general
life-revelation, which is already at hand organically in the church,
the life-giving body of Jesus Christ'.[9]

Following from this, Nevin opposed the fallacy of a conflict
between the spiritual and the material, between outward forms
and inward faith. The outward and inward can never be divorced
without peril to the Christian faith. 'We have no right to set the
inward in opposition to the outward, the spiritual in opposition
to the corporeal, in religion'.[10] The incarnation is the test of all
sound Christianity and so to be real the human must externalize
its inward life in the liturgy.

The Eucharist as the heart of Reformed doctrine

The Eucharist, he argued, is 'in some sense central to the whole
Christian system.' Christianity is grounded in a living union
between Christ and the believer, which great fact is concentrated
in the Lord's Supper.[11] The sacramental controversy of the sixteenth
century was not incidental, for 'it belonged to the innermost
sanctuary of theology'.[12] Any theory of the Eucharist will be found
to accord closely with a corresponding view of the nature of the
union between Christ and his people. The sacramental theology
of the early Reformed church is inseparably connected with the
idea of a living union between Christ and believers in which they
are incorporated into his very nature. This is not simply a union
of a common nature due to the incarnation, nor is it merely a
moral union due to inward agreement or friendship. It is more
than just a legal union in which Christ is the representative of

---

9   J. W. Nevin, *The Mystical Presence: A Vindication of the Reformed or
Calvinistic Doctrine of the Holy Eucharist* (Eugene, Oregon: Wipf & Stock,
2000) 4.

10   Ibid., 5.

11   Ibid., 47, 51.

12   Ibid., 47.

his people, nor does it relate only to his divine nature. Instead the Eucharist embodies the actual grace it represents—the very life of Christ himself. 'We communicate in the Lord's supper… with the living saviour himself, in the fulness of his glorified person, made present to us for the purpose by the power of the Holy Ghost'.[13] The legal relation is grounded on the inward, real unity of life. Our interest in Christ's merits is based on a previous interest in his person. Thus we have 'a real communion with the Word made flesh; not simply with the divinity of Christ, but with his humanity also; since both are inseparably joined together in the unity of his person'.[14] Nevin carefully demarcated it from rationalism on the one hand, seen in the anabaptists, and Romanism and Lutheranism on the other.[15]

This is a real presence—it brings the whole person of Christ into communion with the believer. It is also a spiritual presence, not corporeal or material as in Lutheranism or Roman Catholicism. Nevin stresses two points. First, the sacrament has objective force. It is not simply commemorative, nor is it merely a sign or a picture. Faith is the condition of the efficacy of the sacrament but it is not the principle of the power itself; it is purely receptive. Second, the invisible grace of the sacrament is the substantial life of the Saviour himself, particularly in his human nature. This, says Nevin, was the doctrine held by the Reformed confessions and catechisms.[16]

In contrast, the modern Puritan theory had departed from this benchmark. 'In proportion as the sect character prevails it will be found that baptism and the Lord's Supper are looked on as mere outward signs, in the case of which all proper efficacy is supposed to be previously at hand in the inward state of the

---

13   Ibid., 52–3.
14   Ibid., 53.
15   Ibid., 53–5.
16   In this, as his subsequent work was to show, he was correct.

subject by whom they are received'.[17] From this follows the rejection of infant baptism, and the removal of objective efficacy from the Eucharist. The old doctrine has all but been lost and, where restated is opposed as Romish. Nevin lists a whole range of Reformed theologians who had abandoned Reformed doctrine. Jonathan Edwards figures prominently, in comments such as this:

> it is as if a prince should send an ambassador to a woman in a foreign land, proposing marriage, and by his ambassador should send her his picture, and should desire her to manifest acceptance of his suit, not only by professing her acceptance in words to his ambassador, but in token of her sincerity, openly to take or accept that picture, and to seal her profession by thus representing the matter over again by a symbolical action.[18]

In Edwards' conception, Christ is absent, the sacramental action represents him as a proxy, and the relationship between Christ and the faithful is purely contractual and external.

For Edwards, the Lord's supper is a mutual solemn profession of the two parties transacting the covenant of grace and visibly united in that covenant—the Lord Christ by his minister, the communicants being believers. The minister acts in Christ's name and represents him. By him, Christ makes a solemn profession of his part in the covenant of grace, exhibits the sacrifice of his body broken, confirming and sealing his engagement to be their saviour and food and to impart all benefits of his propitiation and salvation. They in eating and drinking the symbols of Christ's body and blood profess their part in the covenant of grace, profess to embrace the promises, receive the atonement, and to receive Christ as their spiritual food. The sacramental elements are a proxy—as Edwards states, like an ambassador presenting

---

17   Nevin, *Mystical Presence*, 101.

18   'On full communion,' in *Works* (New York, 1844), 1:144–5, cited in Ibid., 104–5. .

a picture of a prince to a woman in a foreign land proposing marriage to the prince. Thus, for Edwards, the Eucharist is merely symbolic, grounded in a contractual theory of covenant.[19] As Nevin says we are 'in another spiritual element entirely... Calvin could not possibly have approved what appears to be the sacramental doctrine of Edwards', for 'according to the old Reformed doctrine the invisible grace of the sacrament includes a real participation in his person'.[20]

For John Dick, the bread and wine are no more than signs designed to denote the benefits that result from the death of Christ. Christians derive no benefit beyond a remembrance of the merits of Christ. All that occurs is that the sufferings of Christ are apprehended by our minds. It would be of no advantage to us to have communion with the body and blood of Christ. Calvin, in his teaching, was incomprehensible.[21]

Nevin concludes, 'the modern Puritan view utterly repudiates [the classic Reformed view], as semi-popish mysticism. It will allow no real participation of Christ's person in the Lord's Supper'.[22]

The differences between the classic Reformed position and 'Puritanism' according to Nevin:

(1) The old Reformed view attributed to the Eucharist something different from all other common exercises of worship. This was so right up to the time of the Westminster Confession of Faith and John Owen. On the other hand, later thought (e.g., John Dick) held that Christ was present in all his ordinances in the same manner.

(2) The old Reformed view held the sacrament to be a mystery beyond our comprehension (Calvin, the French and Scots Confessions, Belgic Confession, Owen). The 'Puritan' view held

19   Jonathan Edwards, 'On full communion,' in *Works* (New York, 1844) 1:145–146.

20   Nevin, *Mystical Presence*, 111.

21   Ibid., 107–8.

22   Nevin, *Mystical Presence*, 118.

it to be completely intelligible to the humblest capacity and rejected Calvin as incomprehensible.

(3) The Reformed view attributed objective force to the sacrament, the reality (Christ) being exhibited and conveyed by the Spirit to the faithful. The 'Puritan' view held the sacrament to ratify a covenant in which God's blessings are conditional on our meeting our obligations.

(4) The Reformed view entailed a real participation in Christ's person, the life of Christ being made present to the faithful. For the 'Puritan' view there is moral union only. At best, the graces of the faithful communicant are called into exercise, while they meditate on his benefits. For Calvin it was Christ first, then his benefits, for the greatest benefit of all is Christ.

Nevin insisted that the Reformed position is that of the early church, the 'Puritan' view of yesterday. Furthermore, he argued, the historical development of transubstantiation is explicable only on the prior existence of the Reformed position; it could hardly have emerged out of the low view of the sacraments with which many are satisfied at present. 'If Christianity had not included in its very nature the idea of a true substantial union with the human life of Christ...such a superstition as that maintained by the church of Rome could never have come to prevail.'[23] Indeed, 'the gross errors of transubstantiation and the sacrifice of the mass, only serve to show more impressively the truth of the position now insisted upon; that the sacrament was felt, from the beginning, to involve not simply a memorial of Christ's sacrifice, but the very power of the sacrifice itself.'[24]

Influences on Nevin and his opponents
Biological categories were coming to replace juridical and mechanistic models. Nevin was influenced here by Herder and

23   Ibid., 122.
24   Ibid., 129.

the early Romantics, and to some extent by Hegel. The idea of organism is pervasive in his writings. The life-principle in the church he often compared to the development of an oak tree out of an acorn. His theology of re-organism was based on the life principle of the second Adam permeating his body, the church. Perhaps because of these influences Nevin can appear rather fuzzy round the edges when it comes to clear doctrinal commitments. Matters such as the atonement and justification, election and the doctrine of Scripture were not of major interest to him. This gave ammunition to Hodge and his friends and led to a widespread belief that Nevin would end up in Rome. These thoughts were unfounded, for Nevin was a self-confessed Calvinist, expressly loyal to the great Reformed confessions, but there is little doubt that his incarnational theology did not adequately integrate the main theological concerns of other Reformed thinkers.

On the other hand, Nevin's opponents, Hodge most conspicuously, but also others who in the ensuing years attacked Calvin's treatment on the Lord's Supper—such as William Cunningham and Robert L. Dabney—were strongly rationalist in their theology. Hodge, as many in nineteenth century America, was indebted to Scottish common sense realism; the degree to which this is so has been a matter of debate. Doctrine must be amenable to common sense, according to this line of thought. Anything that had a vestige of mysticism was to be avoided. Calvin and Nevin were beyond the bounds of right reason.

It is of some note that reverence for tradition (the past teaching of the church) was proposed by a range of Nevin's contemporaries; the Tractarians in England and by Gerlach in the Prussian General Synod of 1846, the latter fighting for recognition of the ancient creeds as the basis for all Christianity. It is very possible that Nevin drew inspiration from these sources. Not only did all these groups share an interest in the Lord's Supper but so, rather interestingly, did the Plymouth Brethren, who were emerging at this time, many of their leaders drawn from high-church Anglicanism.

The sequel

The Mystical Presence was either ignored or attacked in America. James Hastings Nicholl thought this illustrated the anomalous nature of American Christianity when set in the wider context of world Christianity. Hodge attempted to refute it in the *Princeton Review* in April 1848. That summer Nevin wrote a series of articles defending his position in *The Weekly Messenger*, an organ of the German Reformed Church. After a reply by Hodge, pointing in support to Zwingli and the Zürich theology, Nevin wrote an article of over 100 pages, 'The Doctrine of the Reformed Church on the Lord's Supper' in *The Mercersburg Review* in 1850, expanding on his previous work and demonstrating Hodge's position to be historically indefensible. Hodge never replied. Nevin's article was not superseded for a century. In this article, he criticizes Calvin for considering that the human body of Christ is limited in space and time; Nevin, while critical of the peculiar Lutheran Christology, displays a certain affinity with it in the sense that he claims that the life force of Christ's body is not materially bound.

American Christianity was scandalized since, in its eyes, all this implied on Nevin's part a predilection for Rome. The 1840s had seen violent anti-Catholic riots, especially against Irish immigrants. Catholicism was, it was feared, going to undermine the American way of life, founded as it was believed to be on a clear commitment to Protestantism. On the other side of the fence, Roman Catholic newspapers organized campaigns of prayer for Nevin's conversion. The Dutch Reformed Church stopped sending fraternal delegates to the German Reformed Church in 1853, since continuation 'would seem to sanction sentiments favourable to Rome.' The South Carolina classis withdrew from Synod until it purged itself of 'Romanizing heresies.' Some ministers left the denomination. Others protested vehemently. By 1854 Nevin was forced to affirm the Mercersburg theology to be incompatible with Rome. Thereafter he faded into the shadows, suffering from burnout after a decade and a half of intense activity in seminary, college, church, and writing, together with a wife and eight children for whom to care, besides an extended family as well. As it is, he suffered from chronic and painful digestive problems. His main contribution in the rest of his life was liturgical reform in the German Reformed church. At his funeral, A.A. Hodge described him as one of the few great theologians of the Presbyterian church.[25]

HIS INFLUENCE

Ironically, outside his own denomination, which even in the nineteenth century was a small and obscure backwater, Nevin has achieved his greatest impact in the last thirty years. A renewed interest in his theology has developed. It has been particularly influential with advocates of the Federal Vision. Others have been drawn to his churchly, sacramental theology, recognizing that he was correct in his assessment of the classic Reformed teaching, and fearing the impact of the unbridled individualism of American Christianity. *The Mystical Presence* was reprinted in 2000 by Wipf and Stock, a critical biography was published by Daryl Hart in 2005, and Nevin has been discussed sympathetically but also critically by William Evans, in his important book *Imputation and Impartation.*

The main questions thrown up by Nevin, to my mind, surround the relationship between the extrinsic elements of the gospel, the work of Christ in atonement and justification, on the one hand, and the transformative elements, in union with Christ.

25   Hart, *Nevin*, 226. Hart provides full details of Nevin's life and career.

These had become bifurcated and remain so, with a fixation in Reformed circles on the beginning of the Christian life at the expense of its ultimate goal, on the cross in virtual isolation from the incarnation, on the juridical more than the personal, on what is susceptible to reason to the detriment of the mystical and, of course, on the individual at the expense of the church. With this latter focus, the idea of nurture in the church and family, from baptism through catechetical instruction, to the ministry of the Word and the Eucharist has been lost in the search for dramatic crisis experiences.

Nevin sought to do justice to union with Christ; in this he represented a faithful reflection of Calvin. However, there is little doubt, as Evans observes, that he failed adequately to reflect the forensic aspects of salvation, making the new state of the believer determinative, subordinating imputation to impartation.[26] For him, life had priority over doctrine; this was the hallmark of liberalism. His doctrine of justification moves close to the Roman Catholic one. Moreover, his incarnational stress led him to argue that in the incarnation Christ assumed into union a fallen, but sinless, human nature; and produced a universalizing tendency, seen in a visceral opposition to limited atonement. He de-emphasized the written and preached Word; there is thus a bifurcation with the living Word. He misread Calvin insofar as for him there was no competition between the ministry of the Word and the sacraments, or between the sacraments and predestination.

However, with those caveats safeguarded, his insistence on the vital centrality of the incarnation, the church as the locus of salvation and a recovery of the Reformed doctrine of the Eucharist are matters that should be heard and heeded today.

26   W. B. Evans, *Imputation and Impartation: Union with Christ in American Reformed Theology* (Eugene, Oregon: Wipf & Stock, 2009) 183.

12

KARL BARTH (1886–1968)

LIFE AND WORK

Born into a Swiss theological family, conservative pietist in its churchmanship. When he was three his father was appointed Professor of New Testament and Early Church History at the University of Berne.[1] This did not prevent Karl becoming a gang leader and engaging in frequent street fights. The leader of a rival gang later became a Professor of Dogmatics at the University of Berne.[2] Karl often clashed with his teachers, while one school report warned that he needed to pay attention in the religious education class.[3]

He studied at Berne, Berlin, Tübingen, and Marburg under the leading liberals of the day—Adolf von Harnack (1851–1930)

1 See Thomas F. Torrance, *Karl Barth: An Introduction to His Early Theology 1910–1931* (London: T&T Clark, 2000), 15.

2 Eberhard Busch, *Karl Barth: His Life from Letters and Autobiographical Texts* (London: SCM, 1975), 20, 25.

3 Busch, *Barth*, 25.

and especially Johann Wilhelm Hermann (1846–1922). After a time helping Martin Rade edit *Die Christliche Welt* he became pastor of the German Reformed Church in Safenwil (1911–1921), marrying in 1913. During the course of his ministry his theology began to change. He began as a liberal, with a stress on ethics, and the perfectability of man. At first his sermons focussed on ethics, on the need to think seriously about oneself. The ten commandments sometimes said too much and at other times too little, he claimed.[4] Later, in 1935, when he returned to preach one time at Safenwil, he reflected on what he considered to be his pastoral failure. 'I can see now that I did not preach the gospel clearly enough to you during the time when I was your pastor. Since then I have often thought with some trepidation of those who were perhaps led astray or scandalized by what I said at that time.'[5]

A number of factors conspired to alter his attitude. One was the condition of the workers. He was involved in the Christian socialist movement. Barth spearheaded pressure on wealthy industrialists (the most prominent of whom were in his congregation and who he deeply offended) to improve working conditions. He joined the Social Democratic Party, backed strike action, advocated factory legislation and insurance, and became known as 'the red pastor'. Secondly, and most significantly, he was profoundly affected by the outbreak of the First World War on 1 August 1914 and its devastating continuance, which shattered liberalism's claims of the essential goodness of human nature, and the progress of civilization. Most shocking of all for Barth was a declaration in support of German war aims, published the day war broke out, signed by 93 German intellectuals, some of whom were his former teachers. He remarked, 'For me it was almost worse than the violation of Belgian neutrality. And to my dismay, among the signatories I discovered the names of almost all my German teachers (with

4   Busch, *Barth*, 54.
5   Cited in Busch, *Barth*, 64.

the honourable exception of Martin Rade).'[6] Barth regarded their theology as hopelessly compromised. Their ethical failure reflected on their exegesis and dogmatics.[7]

This led Barth, in conversation with his friend Eduard Thurneysen, to a reevaluation of everything he had believed. Over the next few years he came to a number of new positions. One was the supremacy and centrality of God. In this connection he saw God as 'wholly other', not compromised by being domesticated by human culture. The ethical progress of man was no longer central. Rather, revelation was the key. Since this God was not at the whim of man, his revelation was beyond human control and did not depend on anything in human culture. It intersected our world only tangentially, leaving in its wake a metaphorical crater as witness. Barth had read and digested Kant and was also exploring Kierkegaard and forms of existentialism. At the same time, his development brought him to place more reliance on the Bible and it was through a detailed study of *Romans* that his thought crystallized.[8]

The dialectical phase[9]

His commentary on Romans was first published in 1919 and went through three editions in the next few years as Barth revised it. It was not an exegetical commentary. One learns very little about Romans from reading it. Rather, it was an extended reflection on the Godness of God, stressing a radical disjunction between God and humanity. It was heavily criticized by the academic establishment, as all threats to the scholarly status quo undergo. However, a number of younger theologians had emerged who also had developed critical attitudes towards liberalism—Barth's

6   Busch, *Barth*, 81.
7   Busch, *Barth*, 81.
8   On this period, see Torrance, *Barth*, 33–47.
9   See Torrance, *Barth*, 48–132.

friend Thurneysen, Emil Brunner, the NT scholar Rudolf Bultmann, and Friedrich Gogarten, with whom Barth had an un-
easy relationship, developing into animosity. Barth's dialectic was
existential, affirming an infinite qualitative distinction between
God and humanity, time and eternity, which paradoxically come
together in Christ. For us, we can have a personal encounter with
Christ. In Christ is God's No to human sin or self-reliance and
his Yes to human faith. God is so beyond our comprehension
that we can only talk about him in ways that appear contradictory. It was well remarked that this book burst like a bomb on
the theological playgrounds of Europe.

Barth was appointed to posts at the University of Göttingen
in 1921, to Munster in 1925, and Bonn in 1930. During this time
the group of dialectical theologians began to unravel as the
theologies of its members departed from one another. Barth's
task at Göttingen was to teach Reformed theology. This led
him into an exhaustive study of Calvin and then the Reformed
scholastics. He encountered the Reformation and its teaching on
the justification and sanctification of the sinner, repentance and
faith.[10] He came to realize that he had failed to give attention to
the incarnation and to the historical rootedness of the Christian
faith.[11] On the other hand, Bultmann had begun his program of
demythologization, by which he reinterpreted what he regarded
as mythological elements of the gospel like the resurrection, and
Gogarten trod an existentialist path. When Gogarten suggested
a new journal they were starting be called *The Word*, Barth
retorted `Better to call it *The Ship of Fools* than this idolatrous
encumbrance.' He was moving permanently away from Kierkegaard. He came to think it important to interact with him but
better not to return to him.[12]

10   Busch, *Barth*, 143.
11   Busch, *Barth*, 173.
12   Busch, *Barth*, 468.

The Church Dogmatics and Barth's further development

In 1927 Barth produced a volume *Die Christliche Dogmatik* (Christian Dogmatics) but then changed course and began in 1932 a project that was still unfinished at his death, *Die Kirchliche Dogmatik* (Church Dogmatics). He realized the earlier project contained vestiges of liberalism. This project grew and grew until it comprised fourteen huge volumes or half volumes in its unfinished state.

Von Balthasar argued that the catalyst for change was his study of Anselm, which he published in 1931.[13] Barth regarded this as his most important work. It was a commentary on Anselm's famous ontological argument, Barth using it to expound the uniqueness of God. He considered this book to be the key to his theology, to the process of thought which he worked out in the Church Dogmatics.[14] He argued that theology is to be shaped by the object of enquiry and its own inherent rationality. This objective order, apprehended in the belief of the historic church, alone provides the basis for talk about God. It represented, Von Balthasar argued, a move from dialectic, with the prominence of paradox and opposition between God and the human race, to analogy. It led to a breach with Brunner who favoured natural theology (the idea that we can talk about God through human reason or culture independently of revelation), a view that was compatible with support for Nazism.

However, McCormack contends that there is a basic continuity in Barth's thought.[15] It is with the modification of the doctrine of election in 1936 that Barth attained consistency in his exposi-

---

13   Hans Urs Von Balthasar, *The Theology of Karl Barth: Exposition and Interpretation* (Edward T. Oakes; San Francisco: Ignatius, 1992), 86–167.

14   Busch, *Barth*, 206, 210; Torrance, *Barth*, 133ff; Karl Barth, *Fides Quaerens Intellectum: Anselm's Proof of the Existence of God in the Context of His Theological Scheme* (Pittsburgh: Pickwick Publications, 1975).

15   Bruce L. McCormack, *Karl Barth's Critically Realistic Dialectical Theology: Its Genesis and Development 1909–1936* (Oxford: Clarendon Press, 1995).

tion of the doctrine of God, McCormack argues.[16] God's being is a being in this particular act of election, God elects to be trinity, to be God in Christ, Christ elects humanity, Christ is elected as man. God's election determines not only the destiny of humanity but the identity of God. This is an entire recasting not only of election but of the doctrine of God—in fact the whole of theology—in a Christocentric and eternal decision.

The struggle with Hitler

Barth was dismissed from his post at Bonn in 1935. This followed his refusal to give the Hitler salute at the start of classes—he opened with prayer and the singing of a psalm or chorale—his refusal to take the required oath of allegiance to the Führer, stemming from his insistence on the statement in the Barmen Declaration—which he had drafted—that the church had only one leader, Jesus Christ. Most other theologians and church leaders, including Bultmann, capitulated. He moved to the University of Basle for the rest of his life. He was dismissed on a Saturday, and given the new appointment on the following Monday.

Back in Switzerland during the war, Barth was censored by the government because he was constantly urging his countrymen to resist fascism. He sent many radio messages of sympathy and of prayer to Christians in Germany, Holland, France who were suffering and he led relief work for refugees entering Switzerland, finding shoes, medical attention and housing for them.

Soon after the war had ended, in 1946 Barth found himself back at Bonn. Standing in the rubble of the bomb-ruined Kurfürsten Kloss in Bonn, taken over by the University, Barth—speaking extemporaneously to an audience of German students, suffering the depredations of the war and its devastation—declared 'There

---

16   McCormack, *Barth*, 462.

is only one Lord, and this Lord is the Lord of the world, Jesus Christ,' who he added emphatically, was a *Jew*.[17]

Later life

In his seventies Barth began a prison ministry that lasted until his health broke down shortly before his death, preaching to the prisoners and visiting them in their cells. Some of his prison sermons were published under the titles *Deliverance to the Captives* and *Call for God*.[18] Barth had a lifelong love of the music of Mozart. He began every day with it before turning to his theological work. His last hours were spent in preparing a lecture, speaking on the phone to his godson of the Christian hope, and in prayer. It was in an attitude of prayer that he died peacefully on the night of 9 December 1968. Before discovering his body the following morning, his wife had put a record of Mozart on the gramaphone for him. The funeral service ended with his favourite hymn, 'Now thank we all our God.'[19]

THEOLOGY OF THE CHURCH DOGMATICS

The Bible and the Word of God

Barth starts with the actuality of God's self-revelation in contrast to liberalism and existentialism. Revelation creates faith. Barth was famously negative toward natural theology, the claim that we can work by reason from the natural order to God. In contrast to liberal theology's focus on the goodness of humanity, the Fatherhood of God and ethics, its avoidance and large-scale rejection of the supernatural, Barth affirmed the primacy and supremacy of God and his actions.

The Word of God, according to Barth, takes a threefold form: Christ, the living Word; the Bible, the written word; and

17   Busch, *Barth*, 337.

18   Busch, *Barth*, 414–15.

19   Busch, *Barth*, 498–500.

preaching, the proclaimed Word. But revelation is not under our control. It cannot be located in this or that particular place. As such, the Bible is a witness to revelation, a human witness, an inherently fallible witness. Yet it was authoritative not only as witness to revelation but as the Word of God.

As time progressed Barth developed a closer connection between the Bible and revelation. We can say the Bible is word of God. At the same time it is human and capable of error. In practice, the Bible functioned as authority. So the ecumenical unity of the church is a reality to the extent that the authority of the Bible is valid for it.[20] Barth was sceptical about hermeneutics. He was, he said, 'deeply offended or even considerably amused at learning the fortunes of the 'language event' on the theological market, which I follow attentively (I am inclined to call its most vociferous promoters either the troop of Korah or the international union of garden gnomes).'[21] The real issue as he saw it was not so much the encountering of the witness of Scripture so much as the one to whom Scripture bears witness.[22]

In later volumes, Barth located revelation in the incarnate Christ.He came to see that his commentary on Romans did not do justice to the incarnation, to the reality that the Word became flesh.[23] In recognizing this, he moved towards a position in which the incarnation would assume a dominant role affecting the entire theological spectrum.

The Trinity
Barth's discussion of the trinity has been claimed by some to be probably the most important discussion since Calvin, and

---

20   Busch, *Barth*, 343.
21   Busch, *Barth*, 466.
22   Busch, *Barth*, 466.
23   Karl Barth, *CD*, I/2: 50.

possibly since Augustine. He is largely responsible for an upsurge in writing on the trinity in the years since.

Barth disliked talk about persons due to the modern usage of person conveying ideas that did not reflect the meaning the Fathers had given nor to the teaching of the Bible. Our modern understanding of person—if we can be said to understand it—entails a form of individualism that is foreign to the biblical world and was alien to the debate in the fourth century. Instead he proposed the term *seinsweise* or 'way of being.' This is difficult to duplicate precisely in English and the waters were considerably muddied by the English translator rendering it 'mode of being' which implied that Barth was a modalist, effectively denying the eternal distinctiveness of the three. While there are definite problems with the way Barth considers the Father, the Son, and the Holy Spirit, it is unfair and misleading to paint him with this brush.

Barth approaches the trinity via Christ, whereas the Cappadocians, who were mainly responsible for bringing about a resolution of the fourth century trinitarian crisis had come to their position via the Holy Spirit. The question arises as to whether Barth gave a proper place to the Holy Spirit. He regards the Spirit as the bond of union between the Father and the Son; critics have alleged that this leaves the Spirit as somehow less than personal, as merely the subjective dimension of the work of Christ. Again, Barth's stress is on the unity of God. God is God in threefold repetition, he says. He uses the analogy of revealer, revelation, and revealedness. This seems to do less than justice to the eternal distinctions of the three.[24]

Christology
It is commonly claimed that Barth was Christomonistic, everything refracted through Christ. But, as Bromiley holds, no one

---

24   See Robert Letham, *The Holy Trinity: In Scripture, History, Theology, and Worship* (Phillipsburg: Presbyterian & Reformed, 2004), 271–90.

doctrine dominates his theology, for he examines every area from all kinds of angles in a form of a spiral method, constantly returning to the same themes approached from differing angles. The trinity is central if anything is, not Christology, Bromiley argues.[25]

Notwithstanding, Jesus Christ is the centre from which all else radiates, like spokes on a wheel connecting the rim to the hub. While at Göttingen in 1924–5, Barth discovered the *anhyposta-sia—enhypostasia* dogma propounded by the Fathers and given official status at the second Council of Constantinople in 553. By this it was affirmed that the humanity of Christ exists exclusively in the union established in the incarnation by the eternal Son and so is given personhood by the Son, as the flesh and humanity of the Son of God. There is no separate man or human nature from the Son. The nature of the advance, as McCormack suggests, was to locate revelation in the entire incarnate life of Christ.[26]

Indeed, Christ is the locus of all truth concerning God and humanity. Barth was somewhat reluctant to talk about Christology as such, as the whole point of discussion and thought in this area was as a help towards meeting Christ himself.[27] In this, he steadfastly affirmed the reality of the virginal conception and bodily resurrection of the Lord.[28]

Covenant and creation

Given Barth's doctrine of election and his thorough-going stress on the doctrine of God, together with his opposition to all forms of natural theology, it has frequently been asked whether he gave any intrinsic significance to creation. For Barth, creation is not a

---

25   Geoffrey W. Bromiley, *An Introduction to the Theology of Karl Barth* (Grand Rapids: Eerdmans, 1979).

26   McCormack, *Barth*, 327–28.

27   Busch, *Barth*, 411.

28   Thomas F. Torrance, 'My Interaction with Karl Barth,' in *How Karl Barth Changed My Mind* (Donald K. McKim; Grand Rapids: Eerdmans, 1986), 62.

truth naturally available. History and humanity are what they are because God has assumed historical, creaturely existence in the incarnation. Creation is the external form of covenant. Covenant exists in and for creation, while creation exists for covenant. It would be wrong to think that Barth downplayed creation; his persistent opposition to all docetic views of the resurrection that sought to see it as a purely spiritual reality is proof of that. Rather, his aim was to see the whole of creation and redemption in this Christocentric way.

History, primal history and God's pre, post and supratemporality

When Gordon H. Clark, Fred Kloster and Van Til requested to ask Barth some questions, largely on the historicity and datability of aspects of the gospel, particularly the resurrection of Jesus, he refused both from lack of time and because he considered the exercise futile. Writing to Bromiley, who was acting as an intermediary, he said 'Such a discussion would have to rest on the primary presupposition that those who ask the questions have read, learned, and pondered the many things I have already said and written about these matters. They have obviously not done this, but have ignored the many hundreds of pages in the *C.D.* where they might at least have found out…where I really stand and do not stand.'[29] Perhaps they should have read passages such as *CD* III/2, 437ff. Barth strenuously opposed Bultmann's demythologizing of the virgin birth and resurrection.[30] However, Bromiley refers to many secondary sources and 'the magnitude and depth of their misapprehension and misrepresentation' and wonders 'how obviously intelligent and well-trained scholars can commit such elementary blunders in the face of the clearest possible evidence.'[31]

29   Karl Barth, *Letters 1961–1968* (Geoffrey W. Bromiley; translated and edited by Jürgen Fangemeier; Grand Rapids: Eerdmans, 1981), 7–8, 342–43.

30   Busch, *Barth*, 347.

31   Bromiley, *Karl Barth*, xii.

Barth considered that our time, the time of this world under sin and judgement, is enveloped by God's time. Jesus is man in our time but he is also God. He places us in his own time. Yet the relationship between God's time for us in Christ and the time in which we live here and now is difficult to grasp and, in the end, it is found in the eternal determination in which God elects to be the God he is in Christ. This determination is the subject of our next section.

Election, incarnation and covenant—and the spectre of universalism
In 1936, Barth produced the second half of volume two of his Dogmatics. In this he discussed the doctrine of election. He presented a thorough and comprehensive restructuring of the doctrine. He set it on a Christocentric foundation. Christ is both electing God and elect man. The eternal decree is effectively Christ. Election is the gospel. In election God determines to be God in Christ, to be reprobate for each and every human person, and to elect humanity in Christ. This decision transcends all else.

This proposal raises many questions. Berkouwer asked whether there was any place for a transition from wrath to grace.[32] Oliver Crisp has argued with rigorous logic that such a construction is incoherent. If all are elect in Christ, and justification and atonement are to be grounded in this decree, if there is nothing to be sought about God outside Christ, then it follows that all will be saved. The obvious corollary is universal salvation. However, Barth denied that this followed from what he had written. In this his biblical instincts trumped his theological constructions but the result was logically contradictory.[33]

32   G.C. Berkouwer, *The Triumph of Grace in the Theology of Karl Barth* (London: Paternoster Press, 1956).

33   Oliver Crisp, 'On Barth's Denial of Universalism,' *Themelios* 29, no. 1 (2003): 18–29.

Barth's doctrine of election has many problems, not the least of which is an apparent tendency to undermine the historical character of God's revelation. Moreover, it seems to have had a chilling effect on evangelism and mission, for if all are elect in Christ the urgency of gospel proclamation is necessarily blunted. It is often asked where are the Barthian missionaries; the impact of his theology on the church has hardly led to growth. However, we can say that Barth encouraged Reformed theology to return to its roots, to its position before the Synod of Dort (1618–19), which had to some extent been obscured.[34]

The underlying problem is that everything is refracted through the incarnation, from election throughout. This places atonement, justification and so on in the eternal decision of God to be the trinity. It also has the effect of making revelation to appear to be outside time and the Bible as a human and inherently fallible witness to it.

Cornelius Van Til, a vociferous critic of Barth, claimed that 'Never in the history of the church has the triune God been so completely intertwined with his own creature.'[35] Barth did not recognize himself in Van Til's criticisms. Moreover, Van Til's comments on Barth's Christology raise more questions than they were intended to answer. Barth, he said, had abandoned the traditional doctrine of the two natures of Christ *as separate.*[36] However, Van Til had a crucial point in that Barth's overwhelming doctrine of election effectively locates the incarnation, and so

34 This is not to argue that the neo-orthodox attack on Calvinism as departing from the pure pristine theology of Calvin is correct; it is not and has been shown to be so. It is simply to say that Barth drew renewed attention to the classic Reformed theology and that this in itself is beneficial, although much work has been needed to eradicate erroneous ideas relating to it.

35 Cornelius Van Til, *The New Modernism: An Appraisal of the Theology of Barth and Brunner* ([Nutley, New Jersey]: Presbyterian and Reformed, 1973), 435.

36 Van Til, *The New Modernism*, 442.

the humanity of Christ and all people, in eternity and goes in tandem with Barth's denial of the *logos asarkos* (the Word apart from the flesh).

Miscellaneous snippets

Barth chided those who, in the interests of pressing for equality between men and women, joyfully affirmed Galatians 3:28 whereas 'Paul also said several other things on the relation between men and women which were important and right.'[37] He opposed the installation of a stained glass window in the cathedral at Basle on the basis of the second commandment; the congregation voted not to install the window.[38] On Barthians, Barth commented with ascerbity that if there were any he did not consider himself one of them.[39]

FOR FURTHER READING

Major works

The Epistle to the Romans. London: Oxford University Press, 1933. [First edition, 1919]

Church Dogmatics. 14 vols. Trans. Geoffrey W. Bromiley. Edinburgh: T&T Clark, 1956–77.

Fides Quaerens Intellectum: Anselm's Proof for the Existence of God in the Context of his Theological Scheme (London: SCM, 1960) [1931]

Dogmatics in Outline. New York: Harper & Row, 1959. [1946]

---

37   Busch, *Barth*, 358.
38   Busch, *Barth*, 385.
39   Busch, *Barth*, 375–76, 417.

Life and work
Eberhard Busch. *Karl Barth: His Life from Letters and
    Autobiographical Texts.* London/Philadelphia: SCM/
    Fortress, 1976.

Introductory
Geoffrey W. Bromiley. *An Introduction to the Theology of Karl
    Barth.* Grand Rapids: Eerdmans, 1979.

Theological criticism
Hans Urs von Balthasar. *The Theology of Karl Barth.* New York:
    Anchor, 1972.
G.C. Berkouwer. *The Triumph of Grace in the Theology of Karl
    Barth.* Grand Rapids: Eerdmans, 1956.
Eberhard Jüngel. *Karl Barth: A Theological Legacy.* Philadelphia:
    Westminster Press, 1986.
Bruce McCormack. *Karl Barth's Critically Realistic Dialectical
    Theology: Its Genesis and Development 1909–36.* Oxford:
    Clarendon Press, 1995.

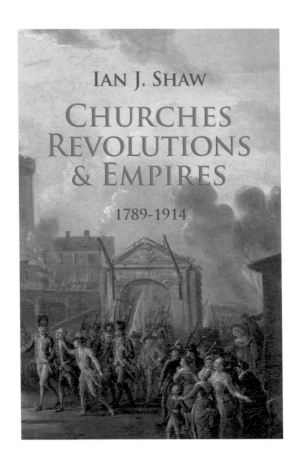

IAN J. SHAW

CHURCHES
REVOLUTIONS
& EMPIRES

1789-1914

ISBN 978-1-84450-774-9

CHURCHES, REVOLUTIONS AND EMPIRES

1789-1914

Ian J. Shaw

"Clear, comprehensive, well-informed about the history of western churches, unusually perceptive about Christian developments elsewhere in the world, and throughout written in entirely accessible prose. Students and experienced readers should both welcome this most helpful volume."

Mark A. Noll,
Francis A. McAnaney Professor of History,
University of Notre Dame, Notre Dame, Indiana

"The book is clear, well arranged and up-to-date in its absorption of recent research. It covers the full range of denominations across the globe, setting religion firmly in its socio-political context and so addressing central historical issues such as empire and national identity. It is likely to command a wide readership in universities, theological colleges, ministers' studies and private homes."

David Bebbington,
Professor of History, University of Stirling, Stirling

"The period from 1789 to 1914 was the crucible in which the modern world was born. A time of revolution, upheaval, empire and war, it shaped Europe and thus the rest of the world. As a result, any understanding of the world today must be built on a clear grasp of what happened during this time."

Carl R. Trueman,
Paul Woolley Professor of Historical Theology and Church History,
Westminster Theological Seminary, Philadelphia, Pennsylvania

"... a sure and illuminating guide to these multiple processes of revolutionary change which began to redraw the contours of world Christianity."

Brian Stanley,
Professor of World Christianity, University of Edinburgh, Edinburgh
and editor of *Cambridge History of Christianity: World Christianities, 1815-1914*

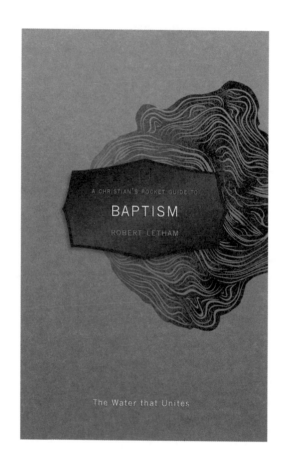

A CHRISTIAN'S POCKET GUIDE TO

BAPTISM

ROBERT LETHAM

The Water that Unites

ISBN 978-1-84550-968-2

A Christian's Pocket Guide to Baptism

The Water that Unites

Robert Letham

It is a 'tragedy', says Letham, that Christians should think of baptism as 'the water that divides'. The sign of our union with Christ should unite Christians, not least because it does not focus on our actions, but on God's mighty deeds. Baptism belongs to him. It must always be administered in connection with faith, yet that does not mean Christians do anything to receive or to earn baptism. They are to be baptized solely because of God's gracious promises.

> "Here is a robust, articulate and biblical presentation of covenant baptism that avoids populism and individualism. Dr Letham has placed baptism in its covenantal and canonical context – a work of God rather than an act of obedience – no bare sign but an active means of grace – for believers and their children."
>
> Liam Goligher,
> Senior Minister, Tenth Presbyterian Church, Philadelphia, Pennsylvania

> "Rightly Letham seeks to understand the issue of baptism within the canonical framework of Scripture. He is hopeful that this is the way forward beyond the impasse that has stymied the church for centuries regarding this precious ordinance .... if you are searching for a well-argued, and irenic, approach to this subject from the vantage-point of infant baptism, this is the book for you."
>
> Michael A. G. Haykin,
> Professor of Church History and Biblical Spirituality,
> The Southern Baptist Theological Seminary, Louisville, Kentucky

Christian Focus Publications

Our mission statement –

STAYING FAITHFUL
In dependence upon God we seek to impact the world through literature faithful to His infallible Word, the Bible. Our aim is to ensure that the Lord Jesus Christ is presented as the only hope to obtain forgiveness of sin, live a useful life and look forward to heaven with Him.

Our books are published in four imprints:

CHRISTIAN
FOCUS

CHRISTIAN
HERITAGE

Popular works including biographies, commentaries, basic doctrine and Christian living.

Books representing some of the best material from the rich heritage of the church.

MENTOR

CF4•K

Books written at a level suitable for Bible College and seminary students, pastors, and other serious readers. The imprint includes commentaries, doctrinal studies, examination of current issues and church history.

Children's books for quality Bible teaching and for all age groups: Sunday school curriculum, puzzle and activity books; personal and family devotional titles, biographies and inspirational stories – because you are never too young to know Jesus!

Christian Focus Publications Ltd,
Geanies House, Fearn, Ross-shire,
IV20 1TW, Scotland, United Kingdom.
www.christianfocus.com